FROM BIRTH TO EIGHTEEN YEARS:

CHILDREN AND THE LAW

By: Siobhan Maclean, Iain Maclean and Mark Shiner

Kirwin Maclean Associates Ltd

City & Guilds name and logo are the registered trade marks of the City and Guilds of London Institute and are used under licence.
"City and Guilds logo © City & Guilds 2002"

From Birth to Eighteen Years: Children and the Law

First Edition: November 2000   ISBN: 1-0-3575-01-X
Second Edition: March 2001   ISBN: 1-903575-09-5
Third Edition: 2005   ISBN 1-903575-29-X
Fourth Edition: 2005   ISBN: 1-903575-38-9
Fifth Edition: 2006   ISBN: 978-1-903575-46-8
Sixth Edition: 2008   **ISBN: 978-1-903575-53-6**

A catalogue record for this book will be available from the British Library

Kirwin Maclean Associates Ltd, 47 Albion Street, Rugeley, Staffs
All Rights Reserved

ISBN: 978-1-903575-53-6
Printed in Great Britain by Kirwin Maclean Associates Ltd

Contents

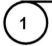 # THE BRITISH LEGAL FRAMEWORK

It is worth having some idea of the way that law comes about. There are a number of different types of "legislation" – including Acts, Regulations etc and a clear relationship between policy and legislation. This chapter will help to clarify these issues.

It should be noted that British law involves four countries (England, Wales, Scotland and Northern Ireland). The Scottish legal system is very different to that of England and Wales. On the whole, the legal framework of Northern Ireland is very similar to the English and Welsh framework.

At present the primary legislation (Acts) that relates to Wales is very similar to legislation that relates to England. However, there could be increased divergence as the Welsh Assembly starts to introduce its own Assembly Measures (Acts that relate to Wales only).

Most legislation is the result of an Act of Parliament. This is usually introduced by the Government of the day and voted upon within the two Houses of Parliament, often being amended as it goes through. At this point it is called a Bill. A Bill becomes an Act once it has passed through Parliament and been given Royal Assent.

Generally a number of stages are gone through before a Government introduces proposed legislation to Parliament. These stages form part of a period of proposal and consultation. This usually starts with what is known as a *Green Paper* - a paper which the Government puts out in order to test public opinion. An example is the Green Paper "Every Child Matters", published in 2003.

Alternatively, the Government can ask a committee or an individual to produce a report following research and investigation into the area in question. For example, The Griffiths Report proposed the structure of community care which was ultimately laid down in the NHS and Community Care Act 1990.

Following the Green Paper a *White Paper* is often published. This is a statement of what the proposed legislation will cover. It usually lays out the philosophy and general principles of the legislation. It is important to be clear that not all Green Papers are followed by a White Paper and not all White Papers lead to an Act of Parliament.

However, not all Acts of Parliament are proposed by the Government. Some start off as *Private Members Bills.* These are introduced into Parliament by individual MPs. One example of this is the Carers (Equal Opportunities) Act 2004.

Acts of Parliament sometimes contain powers which allow the Government to introduce the Act over a period of time. Therefore just because an Act has been passed it does not necessarily mean that everything in it is current law. For Example, the Human Rights Act 1998 was not implemented until October 2000, a full two years after it received Royal Assent.

Acts of Parliament often include a clause which gives the senior minister involved (usually called the Secretary of State) the power to introduce regulations at a later date. These regulations detail more specific law on areas covered by the Act. This is done by means of *Statutory Instrument* which goes before Parliament but is not usually debated. An example of this is the Children Act 1989 which is supplemented by many regulations.

Since devolution, the Welsh Assembly Government has had the power and responsibility to make regulations to support Acts that have gone through Westminster. Often therefore there are regulations that cover a very similar area of practice (eg: leaving care) but the English and Welsh regulations are specific to their own home country. Wherever possible we have made clear the national differences but staff working in Wales are advised to check with their employer about the exact regulations they work under. In a book of this size, it is not always possible to give an overview of all relevant regulations and guidance.

In addition, major pieces of law may be followed at a later date by Guidance or Codes of Practice. These do not have the same force of law, but they explain and clarify the law and offer guidance on good practice. They should therefore be followed by practitioners.

Very often new legislation amends or replaces previous Acts of Parliament, some major pieces of legislation encompass all areas and replace all previous Acts. For example, the Children Act 1989 replaced all previous legislation.

Since 1989 the Children Act has been successively amended. The Children (Leaving Care) Act 2000 inserts nearly all of its sections into the Children Act 1989. In many ways therefore the duties to support care leavers are located in the Children Act 1989.

Staff need to be aware that policy is also a major factor in the way services develop. In many ways, legislation is only one of the ways that policy can be pursued and applied. Other ways that policy can be pursued are by the Government making additional money available if certain targets are met or through the relevant department exercising a leadership role. In origin, the Surestart initiative and Children's Centres were all fuelled by money. It is a number of years since the initiative started and only now has legislation been enacted to 'confirm' the initiative. On the whole local authorities and NHS authorities are under a duty to follow the directions sent out by the relevant Government department.

The creation of Children Trusts is an example of policy being the driving force behind legislation. The Government wants Children's

Trusts to be established and therefore has introduced legislation to facilitate this (The Children Act 2004). The 2004 Act also enables the Secretary of State to insist Children's Trusts are established in an area, if s/he considers the establishment of Children's Trusts to be necessary.

It should be clear by this stage that "Law" therefore, covers a range of areas. In addition to this, there is case law – where a case is taken to a court, the court may make a judgement which interprets the law and sets a precedent.

Having a clear understanding of "the law" is therefore about more than knowing about Acts of Parliament – as the following diagram shows the range of legislation.

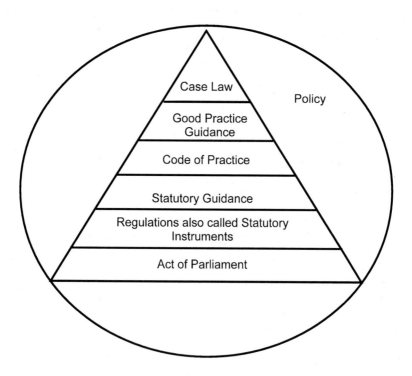

We have tried to cover a range of the different types of legislation in this book. Examples of each 'layer' include:

○ Acts of Parliament – one example is The Children Act 2004. We have tried to cover all the relevant Acts of Parliament in this book. We have also detailed a few Bills which are currently going through Parliament.

○ Regulations – one example would be employment equality regulations – a number of which are covered in Chapter 4.

○ Statutory Guidance – an example would include the guidance on permissible forms of Control in Children's residential care (see Chapter 11).

○ Code of Practice – The Mental Health Act 1983 has an associated Code of Practice. The Care Standards Act 2000 places a responsibility on the GSCC to issue a code of practice for social care workers. Codes of Practice are referred to where relevant in the book.

○ Good Practice Guidance – the Government issues a range of good practice guidance which changes regularly. Since there is so much good practice guidance, we have not covered this in the book but staff should make sure that they are familiar with the good practice guidance relevant to their area of practice.

○ Case Law – one example of the impact of case law on work with children and young people is the Fraser ruling (see Chapter 5).

○ Policy – in December 2007 the Government published The Children's Plan. This clarifies government policy in terms of children's services over the coming years (see Chapter 19).

In Summary

This background information is offered to provide you with an understanding of the legislative framework within which you operate. It is not important for you to know about the detail of the complex English and Welsh legal system but a basic understanding will help you to recognise the framework from which the law arises.

(2)   EUROPEAN LEGISLATION

The knowledge specification for the Health and Social Care NVQs states that the staff member needs to know, understand and apply current local, national and European legislation. The inclusion of the reference to European legislation has caused a great deal of uncertainty for assessors and anxiety for NVQ candidates.

This chapter should help to clarify issues around European legislation.

Member states of the European Union (EU) have agreed that EU directives, in various subject areas, have to be applied to member states' own laws. Areas in which the EU has the legislative lead, through directives, include:

O   employment law and workers rights (especially equality of opportunity)

O   health and safety in the workplace

O   business activities and trade

O   consumer rights

O   free movement of labour across the EU

O   aspects of public health (communicable diseases)

The EU requires that member states translate their Directives into the member states own national laws. The exact wording of the national laws is up to each member state but the shared objectives must be achieved. Member states MUST translate the Directives within certain timescales or face enforcement action from the EU – usually successive official 'telling offs' with the final sanction being a fine applied by the European Court of Justice, (which applies EU law to all member states). It is only in exceptional circumstances that an individual citizen of a member state could invoke an EU directive directly.

In terms of the child care and social care sector, the main impact of EU Directives has been to introduce changes to health and safety law, employment law and laws relating to countering discrimination. Examples of EU Directives that have resulted in changes to British law include:

O   Health and Safety at Work Directive (89/391/EEC) (Framework) resulted in the introduction of the Management of Health and Safety at Work Regulations 1992 (since amended).

O   EU Directive 90/268/EEC (Manual Handling of Loads) resulted in the introduction of the Manual Handling Operations Regulations 1992

O   EU Directive 89/654/EEC (Workplaces) resulted in the introduction of the Workplace (Health, Safety and Welfare) Regulations 1992

- EU Directive 2000/43/EC (Racial Equality) resulted in the introduction of the Race Relations Act 1976 (Amendment) Regulations 2003
- EU Directive 2000/78/EC (Equal Treatment in Employment) has resulted in the:
  - Employment Equality (Sexual Orientation) Regulations 2003
  - Disability Discrimination Act 1995 (Amendment) Regulations 2003
  - Employment Equality (Age) Regulations 2006
- EU Directive 2002/73/EC (Equal Treatment for Men and Women in Employment and Training) has resulted in the Employment Equality (Sex Discrimination) Regulations 2005

 In Summary

Where a unit knowledge specification makes reference to European legislation and/or directives, it is sufficient within the UK to refer to Westminster legislation – as covered in this book. There is no need for you to look any wider since all relevant European legislation will have been translated into British law by Parliament.

3   THE COURT SYSTEM IN ENGLAND AND WALES

In considering the legal system, it is always useful to have an understanding of the court system. Generally speaking there are two distinct Court systems in England and Wales. One covering criminal cases and one dealing with civil matters.

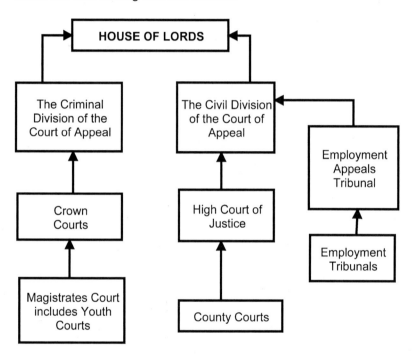

This chapter gives a brief outline of the different courts in this system.

Magistrates Courts

These are sometimes known as the "Court of first instance". Essentially, they are the lowest of the Courts in England and Wales. They deal principally with criminal matters and the jurisdiction of the Magistrates is limited. Therefore, they deal predominantly with less serious offences or they refer people on to Crown Court.

Youth Courts

The 1991 Criminal Justice Act renamed the old Juvenile Courts and Juvenile Court Panels as "Youth Courts" and "Youth Court Panels". The Youth Court was given something of a procedural makeover with the presiding magistrates given specific training. The Youth Court deals with young people up to and including the age of 17.

Crown Courts

These deal with more serious criminal cases and appeals from Magistrates Courts. They involve a judge and jury and are the traditional view of Courts.

County Courts

These Courts act as the first point of call for civil cases. They operate on an area basis and are normally presided over by circuit judges or registrars.

High Court of Justice

This Court deals with more high profile and complex civil matters. Cases here are heard by a High Court Judge. There are three divisions of the High Court.

a) The Queens Bench – this division deals with issues of contract and supervises lower Courts and tribunals.
b) The Chancery Division – this division deals with a range of matters including wills and bankruptcy.
c) The Family Division – this division deals with family matters e.g.: divorce matters, matters relating to children etc.

Court of Appeal

This Court has two divisions:

a) Civil – this hears appeals from County Courts and the High Court of Justice.
b) Criminal – this hears appeals from the Crown Court.

The House of Lords

The House of Lords hears appeals on important legal issues from the Court of Appeal and (rarely) from the High Court. These issues are heard by the Law Lords.

Tribunals

In addition to the Court system outlined there are also a variety of employment tribunals. Tribunals deal with a range of employment issues including those involving industrial relations, equal pay and sex discrimination. They consist of a legally qualified chairperson (appointed by the Lord Chancellor) and two lay members – one from a managerial background and one from a trade union.

In Summary

It is not important to have a detailed understanding of the court system but it is always useful to place an understanding of legislation into the context of the Court system.

(4) ANTI-OPPRESSIVE PRACTICE

In Great Britain we have a history of legislation designed to ensure that discrimination on certain grounds is unlawful. It is important to know about this legislation and to develop an understanding of the way in which this applies to your work setting, in order to enhance your own practice in terms of combating oppression. However, be warned that good practice is way ahead of the minimum legal requirements.

If you think of anti-oppressive practice as a bag of tools then the legal framework is one tool to aid your practice. There are two other good reasons to be aware of what the law says in this area – firstly, you are required to work within the law. Secondly, you need to be aware of what action could be taken if any of the people you work with have been oppressed and wish to take legal action.

This chapter will cover:

- Sex Discrimination Act (SDA) 1975
- Equal Pay Act 1970/1975
- Race Relations Act (RRA) 1976
- Public Order Act 1986
- Children Act 1989
- Disability Discrimination Act 1995
- Education Act 1996
- Crime and Disorder Act 1998
- Race Relations (Amendment) Act 2000
- Special Educational Needs and Disability Act 2001
- Disability Discrimination Act 2005
- Equality Act 2006

in addition to relevant Regulations.

Sex Discrimination Act 1975

Definitions of discrimination are vital in terms of understanding and operating this piece of legislation. This Act makes it unlawful to discriminate on the grounds of gender.

Discrimination is set out into two forms – direct and indirect.

Direct Discrimination is quite straightforward. Simply stated it means that one person is treated less favourably than another based on gender. If a woman, for example, is treated less favourably than a man because of typical, stereotyped views about the role of women in society, that could amount to direct discrimination. One example of this would be if a woman is refused a pint of bitter in a public house and told that they only serve half pints to women.

Indirect Discrimination is more complex. It takes place if a requirement or condition is imposed which, on the face of it, is nothing to do with gender but in practice is such that, for example, the proportion of women who can comply with it is considerably less than the proportion of men who can comply with it. For example, a height requirement for a job may be classed as indirect discrimination if it would exclude women from applying.

The Sex Discrimination Act also makes it unlawful to discriminate on the ground of marital status.

A number of statutory exemptions apply under the Act – for example, charitable bodies are able to confer benefits on members of one sex only.

The Act does allow for positive action. For example, where being of a particular sex is a genuine occupational qualification. Positive action may, for example, mean advertising for a male member of staff to work with men where personal care is involved.

This Act established the Equal Opportunities Commission, which has now been replaced by the Equality and Human Rights Commission – see Equality Act 2006.

As a result of various European Union Directives, the Sex Discrimination Act 1975 has been progressively amended. The

Employment Equality (Sex Discrimination) Regulations 2005 have made various changes so that, in respect of employment and training:

○ harassment, including sexual harassment, on the grounds of a person's gender is made unlawful
○ discrimination on the grounds of pregnancy or maternity leave is classified as unlawful sex discrimination
○ Commission is given the duty to work towards the elimination of harassment (in addition to its pre-existing duties)

The Equality Act 2006 inserted a general duty on public authorities into the 1975 Act. This new duty is:

○ In carrying out their functions, public authorities must have due regard to the need
  - to eliminate unlawful discrimination and harassment
  - promote equality of opportunity between men and women

Equal Pay Act 1970

This Act was passed in 1970 but did not come into force until 1975. Essentially, the Act states that men and women should receive equal pay for work of equal value.

Race Relations Act 1976

The Race Relations Act is essentially modelled on the Sex Discrimination Act and even though the issues/problems covered are very different the approaches are very similar.

Once again, this Act uses the terms direct and indirect discrimination. It adds a third type of discrimination – victimisation.

Discrimination by means of victimisation means treating the person less favourably because that person has made a complaint or allegation of discrimination, or has acted as a witness or informant in connection with such an allegation, or intends to do so.

This Act makes discrimination on the grounds of race illegal. Race is defined in terms of colour, race, nationality or ethnic or national origins. It does not cover religion. However, a group of people that have established their own racial identity around their religion may be treated under the Act as a distinct ethnic group. For example, Sikhs have been treated under the Act as a distinct ethnic group.

The areas covered by the Act are education, housing, employment, public and private clubs, entertainment and the provision of goods and services.

This Act set up the Commission for Racial Equality, which has now been replaced by the Equality and Human Rights Commission – see Equality Act 2006.

Once again, this Act allows for positive action in order to encourage members of a particular group to participate if they have been under represented, or to ensure the welfare of a particular group.

This Act has been strengthened by additional sections inserted by the Race Relations (Amendment) Act 2000. Public authorities have a duty, when carrying out their functions, to have due regard to the need to eliminate unlawful discrimination and to promote equality of opportunity and good relations between persons of different racial groups.

As a result of European Union Directive 2000/43/EC (Equal Treatment of People Irrespective of Racial or Ethnic Origin) the Race Relations 1976 (Amendment) Regulations 2003 have made various changes to the 1976 Act. These include:

O   A new definition of harassment on the ground of a person's race, ethnic or national origins

O   It is unlawful for an employer to subject an employee or an applicant to racial harassment

O   It is unlawful for public bodies concerned with the provision of health, welfare or other services to subject persons to harassment

O   A re-definition, but continued recognition, that being of a particular race, ethnic or national origin can be a determining requirement for a particular employment

Public Order Act 1986

This Act sets out the law relating to *incitement to racial hatred.* Section 18 covers the use of words or gestures and section 19 covers publishing or distributing written material. The Act also covers the performance of plays, broadcasting (sound or vision) and the possession of racially inflammatory material (Vernon 1993).

Children Act 1989

For the first time this Act has required local authorities to consider a child's race, religion, culture and linguistic background before making any decisions about a child, for example, before placing the child in either day, foster or residential care.

All child care services are required to give due consideration to the race, culture and language of the children living in the area. Approval of registration can be withheld if these criteria are not met.

This Act has, as its centre, the Paramountcy Principle that must be considered by any authority when making a decision about a child, either in Court or in the care of the local authority. This places the welfare of the child including its racial and cultural needs, as paramount over any other consideration. This overrides even the wishes of parents and in particular cases, overrides racial and cultural issues. The "Welfare Checklist" (s.1) contains this principle whilst also directing that the child's 'background' must be taken into consideration when making decisions. More specifically, under the General Duties of the local authority in relation to any child looked after by them: 'religious persuasion, racial origin, cultural and linguistic background' must be considered (s.22).

It should be noted that the paramount Welfare Principle always takes precedence. For example, the Act states that under section 8 a court may make a "Prohibited Steps Order" which is commonly used to stop a parent taking a child out of the country, perhaps to that parent's country of origin, if it is seen to be against the child's welfare. The child may be completely socialised as British, for example, and may not fully identify with the parent's country of origin.

Disability Discrimination Act 1995

This Act creates legally enforceable rights for people with disabilities. It makes it unlawful to discriminate against people with disabilities in employment, access to goods, services, transport and education.

The Act defines a disabled person as someone who has:-

"A physical or mental impairment which has a substantial and long term adverse effect on (their) ability to carry out normal day-to-day activities"

This Act does state that in terms of people with a disability and employment some discrimination may be "*justifiable*". The introduction of this concept of justification into direct discrimination in this Act is in marked contrast to both the Sex Discrimination Act and the Race Relations Act where direct discrimination is incapable of justification.

The Disability Discrimination Act (DDA 1995) has been significantly strengthened by the Special Educational Needs and Disability Act 2001.

The amendments relate to schools and colleges. New sections have been inserted into the DDA 1995. These include:-

O Section 28A this makes it unlawful for a school to discriminate against a disabled person (e.g. a prospective pupil).

O Discrimination of a pupil is defined as treating someone "for a reason which relates to his disability, it treats him less favourably than it treats or would treat others to whom that reason does not or would not apply and it cannot show that the treatment in question is justified".

Crown Copyright

O Section 28C requires schools to ensure that disabled pupils are not placed at a substantial disadvantage in comparison with persons who are not disabled.

O Section 28D requires local education authorities to prepare accessibility strategies and plans. One aspect of these plans must include improving the physical environment of schools for the purpose of enabling disabled pupils to take advantage of educational services.

O Section 28H establishes the Special Educational Needs and Disability Tribunal. Pupils who feel they are discriminated against unlawfully because of their disability can make a claim to the Tribunal.

O Additional sections make it unlawful for Further and Higher Education Colleges to discriminate against a disabled student, both in terms of admissions in the first place and educational opportunities once enrolled (s.28R, 28S, 28T etc).

The Disability Discrimination Act 2005 inserted additional sections into the DDA 1995. Some of these sections introduced new duties onto public authorities. These duties are that in carrying out their functions public authorities are to have due regard to:

O The need to eliminate discrimination against people with disabilities that is unlawful

O The need to eliminate harassment that is unlawful

O The need to promote equality of opportunity between disabled persons and other persons

O The need to take steps to take account of disabled person's disabilities, even where that involves treating disabled person's more favourably than other persons.

This Act still allows for situations where discrimination is justifiable, but the impression is this should be in exceptional circumstances only (eg. disproportionate costs involved).

Education Act 1996

This Act states that a syllabus of religious education must reflect the principle that religious traditions in the UK are in the main Christian, while taking into account the other principal religions represented in Great Britain. Parents can withdraw their children from school religious education to receive it elsewhere. Alternatives can be facilitated but do not have to be funded by the schools' governing body.

The Special Educational Needs and Disability Act 2001 has inserted a strengthened section 316 into the Education Act 1996. The new section 316 establishes a "duty to educate children with special educational needs in mainstream schools".

Crown Copyright

The parents of a child with special educational needs have a right to advice and information from the local education authority about their child's needs.

A new section (332B) is also inserted requiring local education authorities to make arrangements to avoid or resolve disagreements between the authority and the parents of a child with special educational needs.

Annual reports made by the county, voluntary, or grant maintained schools must account for their admissions procedures for disabled pupils. The report must also detail measures taken to avoid discrimination against disabled pupils, and facilities for access.

Crime and Disorder Act 1998

Section 28 of this Act defines what a racially aggravated offence is. In short, this is any offence where the offender demonstrates, at any point, that their hostility toward the victim is based upon the victim's perceived membership of a racial group. This includes harassment.

Race Relations (Amendment) Act 2000

This Act amends the Race Relations Act 1976. All the sections of the 2000 Act are inserted into the 1976 Act.

Special Educational Needs and Disability Act 2001

The major provisions of the Special Educational Needs and Disability Act 2001 are inserted into either the Education Act 1996 or the Disability Discrimination Act 1995.

Part 1 of this Act results in Part 4 of the Education Act 1996 being significantly amended. This includes:

○ The right of children with SEN to be educated in mainstream schools is strengthened. This right is dependent on parents wanting their child to enter mainstream school and the interests of other children being protected.

O   Local Education Authorities (LEA's) have to provide parents of children with SEN with advice, information and a means of resolving disputes with schools and LEA's.

Part 2 of the 2001 Act inserts a number of sections into the Disability Discrimination Act 1995. New duties are placed on all schools and LEA's:

O   Not to treat disabled pupils less favourably, without justification, for a reason which relates to disability.

O   To make reasonable adjustments so that disabled pupils are not put at a substantial disadvantage compared to pupils who are not disabled.

O   There is a duty to plan strategically and make progress in increasing accessibility to schools premises and to the way the curriculum is presented.

New duties are placed on further and higher education institutions. Therefore further education colleges:

O   Are under a duty not to treat disabled students less favourably, without justification, for a reason which relates to their disability.

O   Are under a duty to make reasonable adjustments to ensure that people who are disabled are not put at a substantial disadvantage compared to people who are not disabled in accessing further, higher (and LEA adult education).

Disability Discrimination Act 2005

The Disability Discrimination Act 2005 inserted additional sections into the Disability Discrimination Act 1995. Some of these sections relate to public authorities. Many of the sections relate to transport. See the discussion of the Disability Discrimination Act 1995 for the new duties on public authorities.

Equality Act 2006

Each of the main anti-discriminatory Acts, the Sex Discrimination Act 1975, the Race Relations Act 1976 and the Disability Discrimination Act 1995 established their own Commission. However, the equality agenda has widened. Through the European Union new regulations have made the discrimination of people on the grounds of sexual orientation, religion or belief and age unlawful. These new regulations apply to work and training only. Additionally there was no organisation responsible for promoting equality in these new areas. The Government therefore decided to establish a commission responsible for promoting equal opportunities for all. Additionally, although public bodies have to adhere to the Human Rights Act 1998 no public body exists to promote the Human Rights Act. This duty has also been given to the new Commission.

Equality and Human Rights Commission

This Commission is established by s.1 of the 2006 Act. It has a general duty (s.3) to encourage and support the development of a society in which:

a)   people's ability to achieve their potential is not limited by prejudice or discrimination

b)   there is respect for and protection of each individual's human rights

c)   there is respect for the dignity and worth of each individual

d)   each individual has an equal opportunity to participate in society

e)   there is mutual respect between groups based on understanding and valuing of diversity and on shared respect for equality and human rights.

The Commission is to pursue these objectives by:

O   Promoting equality of opportunity and diversity

O   Enforcing anti-discriminatory legislation

O   Promoting awareness, understanding and protection of human rights.

The Commission has the power to:

O   Issue codes of practice to assist organisations to comply with legislation

O   Initiate enquiries and investigations

O   Issue notices requiring people to comply with anti-discriminatory legislation

O   Assist individuals take legal proceedings where anti-discriminatory legislation appears to have been violated

The Equality Act 2006 also makes additional forms of discrimination unlawful. These being:

O   Direct or indirect discrimination against people on the basis of their religion or beliefs (this includes a person who has no beliefs). Areas covered include the provision of goods, facilities, services or property. There are a range of exceptions. Religious organisations can make adhering to their religion a requirement for membership. Religious charities can provide benefits only to people of a specific religion.

O   The Secretary of State is given the power to make regulations which will make discrimination, on the grounds of sexual orientation, unlawful.

O   An additional duty on public authorities is inserted into the SDA 1975 (to promote equality of opportunity between men and women).

The Equality and Human Rights Commission began its work on 1st October 2007 and brought together the previous commissions:

O   Equal Opportunities Commission
O   Commission for Racial Equality
O   Disability Rights Commission

Associated Regulations

Sexual Orientation

The Employment Equality (Sexual Orientation) Regulations 2003 were introduced in response to EU Directive 2000/78/EC (establishing a general framework for equal treatment in employment). The 2003 Regulations make it unlawful to discriminate on the grounds of sexual orientation in the area of employment and training.

Employment Equality in Respect of Religion and Belief

In respect of employment and training the Employment Equality (Religion and Belief) Regulations 2003 make discrimination (direct, indirect or harassment) against a person, because of their religion or belief, unlawful. However there are exceptions allowed within these Regulations in situations where being of a particular religion or belief is a genuine and determining occupational requirement.

Employment Equality in Respect of Age

Through the Employment Equality (Age) Regulations 2006, people cannot be discriminated in work or training on the basis of age. If an employer does introduce an age related condition, there must be an objective work related justification for this. An employer can require staff to retire at the age of 65 but must give them six months notice. The employee has the right to request to continue working. The employer can still decide to retire the employee.

 In Summary

It is important to know about the major pieces of social legislation affecting your practice in this area. However, the law is very limited in scope and best practice is way ahead of legislation.

(5) RIGHTS

Within English and Welsh law it has traditionally been the case that laws introduced by Parliament state what actions or behaviours constitute an offence. In other words the law tells us what we cannot do. The implication of this is that so long as we do not do something that is an offence the action is lawful or we have a right to do it. However, this is only by implication and in effect different people have been treated differently (discriminated against) in all sorts of ways in Britain.

Over the years because of the grey areas in English and Welsh law many people who felt their rights were not upheld in English law took their cases to the European Court of Human Rights. This court enforces the European Convention on Human Rights across all the European Countries that have signed the Convention. Britain is one of these countries. The European Convention states rights positively. It makes clear what our rights are. If we are stopped from exercising one of these rights we can take our claim to the European Court. The European Convention on Human Rights and the work of the Court were so successful that Parliament decided to make the European Convention part of English and Welsh law, through the Human Rights Act 1998.

This chapter will cover:

- Human Rights Act 1998
- Police and Criminal Evidence Act 1984
- Children Act 1989
- National Health Service and Community Care Act 1990
- Carers (Recognition and Services Act) 1995
- Carers and Disabled Children Act 2000
- Carers (Equal Opportunities) Act 2004
- Fraser Judgement
- UN Convention on the Rights of the Child

Human Rights Act 1998

The Human Rights Act 1998 was introduced by Parliament and came into force in October 2000. It is, in effect, the European Convention on Human Rights.

Listed in Schedule 1 of the Act are various rights. These include:

Article 2

Everyone's right to life shall be protected by law.

Article 3

No one shall be subjected to..........degrading........treatment.

Article 5

Everyone has the right to liberty and security of person.

Article 8

Everyone has the right to respect for his private and family life and his correspondence.

Article 9

Everyone has the right to freedom of thought, conscience and religion.

Article 12

Men and women of marriageable age have the right to marry and to found a family.

Article 14

The enjoyment of these rights and freedoms set forth in this Convention shall be secured without discrimination on any ground....

Under Part II The First Protocol of the Act three further articles are listed. One of these relates to the right to education.

Article 2

No person shall be denied the right to education......the State shall respect the right of parents to ensure such education is in conformity with their own religious and philosophical convictions.

Implications of the Human Rights Act 1998

It is still not clear what the impact of this Act will be. It will only be as a result of cases brought before courts in England and Wales that its full implications will be known.

However, there are presently various practices in services that _may_ infringe one or other of the rights listed in the Act. Courts will only make a judgement if an individual, possibly supported by an organisation, takes a claim of infringed or violated rights to the court.

In general it is important to be conscious that any public authority (statutory service) has an obligation under the Human Rights Act to uphold people's rights and not just to avoid infringing a person's rights.

Situations that children's services need to be aware of include:

1) A child or young person is being looked after by a local authority and that child or young person is subjected to continued bullying. If the local authority failed to act assertively it could be argued they failed to uphold the young person's right to be free from degrading treatment (Article 3).

2) A family that is in danger of breaking down. Where this is known to social services and they do not act the family could make a complaint to a court. If the family could argue that social services refusal to provide services meant the family had no support and so the family broke up then the court may say this contravenes Article 8 (right to respect for family life).

3) All looked after children must be able to practice their religion in the way they would have been supported by family. Failure to do this could be seen as violating Article 9 (right to practice own religion). (See Thompson (2000) for further discussion).

These are just three examples but there will probably be many other examples that could arise from the implementation of the Human Rights Act 1998. Services and staff should welcome this Act. It will hopefully lead to raised standards and expectations which will be for the benefit of all.

Other pieces of legislation do positively state a limited number of rights. Whilst we have given brief details here of what rights are contained in the legislation see later chapters for more details on the specific Acts. Some of the rights are relevant to adults but are included here so staff are aware of legislation that may be relevant for care leavers

Police and Criminal Evidence Act 1984

O establishes the rights of all people arrested by the police

O detainees have the right to legal advice (on request) and the right to have the police notify a person who is likely to have an interest in their welfare

O detainees who are minors (under 17 in the original Act) or adults who due to a disability or mental illness are seen as being vulnerable adults are entitled to an "Appropriate Adult" being present

Children Act 1989

O the old concept of "Parental Rights" is removed under this Act and replaced with Parental Responsibility.

O the child has the right to have their wishes and feelings taken into consideration in conjunction with their level of maturity and understanding in relation to parental responsibility and decisions made about their care

O in cases where parental responsibility is shared between several persons, each has the right to make decisions about the child, independently of the other. Local authorities, however, must consult and work in partnership with parents but may act against their wishes if a Care Order or other relevant order has been made

O children have the right to certain services and support after they have left care.

The Children Act details certain rights for children, some of which are dependent on age.

O children have the right to participate in decisions made about them. The extent of their involvement will depend upon their age and understanding

- young people have the right to receive help in preparing themselves for leaving care and to assistance when they have left care

- children defined as "in need" have the right to certain services

- children and young people and/or their parents have a right to complain about services

The right to complain has been enhanced by amendments to the Children Act 1989 introduced through the Adoption and Children Act 2002. Where a local authority becomes aware that a child or person is intending to make a complaint, the local authority must:

- provide the person or child with information about advocacy services

- offer the person or child help in obtaining an advocate

National Health Service and Community Care Act 1990

- adults with social care needs have the right to an assessment of their needs

- individuals have the right to complain

- this Act also attempted to introduce the right of a person to choose which service they received if the assessment had identified that the person needed a service

Carers (Recognition and Services) Act 1995

This applies to all people who act as a principal carer for another person. The Act gives carer's the right to an assessment of their own needs.

However the assessment of the carer's needs must occur at the same time as the assessment of the family member who has social care needs. Young carers can request an assessment of their needs if their family member is being assessed. Young carers could also receive support from social services under section 17 of the Children Act if the young carer's welfare or development might suffer if support is not provided.

Carers and Disabled Children Act 2000

This Act received Royal Assent in July 2000. It introduces six key changes with the intentions of enabling local authorities to offer new support to carers.

1. People who are providing (or are about to provide) regular and substantial levels of care to someone will effectively have an unconditional right to an assessment of their own needs (s.1). This assessment of the carer's needs can occur following their request even if the person cared for is not receiving services and refuses to be assessed. In the Act a carer is defined as someone aged 16 or more caring for someone aged 18 or more who is not being paid or is not contracted as a volunteer.

2. Following the assessment social services can arrange services for the carer or alternatively provide direct payments so that the carer can arrange their own support arrangements instead of receiving services arranged directly by social services. This includes young carers aged 16 or 17.

3. People with parental responsibility for a disabled child and who provide a substantial amount of care on a regular basis for that child have a right to an assessment of their needs as a carer (s.6). (Following the assessment any services that were required to meet identified needs would be provided under s.17 of the Children Act).

4. The Carers and Disabled Children Act (2000) also inserts two new sections 17A and 17B into the Children Act (1989) which enable social services to provide direct payments to the carer so the carer can arrange their own support. Any direct payment would be instead of a service arranged directly by social services.

5. This Act enables social services to run short-break (respite) voucher schemes. This is intended to introduce flexibility into respite provision.

6. This Act enables local authorities to charge carers for the services they receive (s.8).

Carers (Equal Opportunities) Act 2004

This Act covers both England and Wales.

The Act gives carers new rights to information about assessment. It amends previous carers legislation to state that local authorities have a duty to inform carers of their right to an assessment.

Section 2 of the Act states that a carer's assessment must take into account whether the carer works or wants to work, any courses the carer is taking or wants to take and any other leisure activities the carer undertakes or wants to undertake.

The Act also encourages authorities to work in co-operation by giving local authorities new powers to enlist the help of housing, health, education and other local authorities to provide support to carers. If the local authority makes a request to another authority to plan services, that authority must give the request due consideration.

Fraser Judgement

In addition to Acts of Parliament, case law (i.e. where a case has been brought to court and a decision made) has an effect upon English law. One piece of case law which has had a significant impact on children's services in England is what has become known as the Fraser Judgement or Ruling.

The phrase Fraser Judgement refers to a child or young person who has sufficient understanding to make decisions for themselves. It follows the decision in Gillick v West Norfolk and Wisbech Area Health Authority (1986). In this case the House of Lords discussed the relationship between parent and child and the responsibilities arising from this relationship. Although the judgement related to consent to medical treatment the principle applies to decision making on any matter of importance. (Fraser was the principle judge who heard the case).

The judgement indicated that there is a tapering relationship between parents and their children. As children become older and more mature the parent's rights to know about their child's affairs and to make decisions on their behalf, diminishes. The ruling hence means that children do not need to wait for the age of majority to be able to decide matters for themselves - informed decisions can be made at an earlier age.

Brayne and Carr (2003) point out that since 1986 other court cases have established the principle that competent children are able to give consent to treatment but cannot withhold consent. Thus a 16 or 17 year old child is viewed as having limited competence especially where life saving treatment is involved. The welfare of a child can still be decided by others, particularly the court.

United Nations Convention On The Rights Of The Child

In addition to the legal rights outlined, the United Nations has developed a Convention on the Rights of the Child. Essentially, the Convention is an international ethical code. However the Convention is taken very seriously. The Welsh Assembly Government has adopted the Convention as one of its core aims. Since this list of rights applies exclusively to children it is essential that as a member of staff or foster carer you are aware of some of the main provisions.

The UN Convention on the Rights of the Child has 54 articles. Below are some of those most relevant to children's services.

Article 3 Adults should, in all their dealings with you, do what is best for you.

Article 6 Everyone should recognise your right to live.

Article 9 You should not be separated from your parents unless it is for your own good.

Article 10 You have the right to live in the same place and country as your parents.

Article 12 You have the right to give your opinion and be taken seriously on decisions that affect you.

Article 13 You have the right to information and to say what you think unless it breaks the rights of others.

Article 15 You have the right to meet and make friends with other people unless it breaks the rights of others.

Article 16 You have the right to a private life.

Article 18 Both your parents should be involved in bringing you up and do what is best for you.

Article 19 No one should hurt you, not even your parents. You should be protected from abuse, violence and neglect.

Article 20 If you do not live with, or have, parents, you have the right to special protection and help.

Article 21 If you are adopted, everything arranged should be in your best interests.

Article 22 If you are a refugee, you have the right to special protection and help.

Article 23 If you are mentally or physically disabled, you have the right to special care and education.

Article 27 You have the right to a good enough "standard of living" – food, clothes, a place to live etc.

Article 28 You have a right to an education. Primary education must be free.

Article 29 Education should develop your personality, talents, mental and physical abilities, and prepare you to live responsibly and peacefully.

Article 30 If you are from a minority group you have the right to enjoy your own culture, religion and language.

Article 31 You have the right to play.

Article 33 You have the right to be protected from illegal drugs.

Article 34 You have the right to be protected from sexual abuse.

Article 37 Even when in the wrong, no one should punish you in a way that humiliates or hurts you badly.

Article 39 If you are hurt or neglected you have the right to care and treatment.

Article 40 You have the right to defend yourself if accused of a crime.

Article 42 You have the right to learn about your rights.

In Summary

Until recently, issues of rights did not have a high profile within the English and Welsh legislative framework. However, the introduction of the Human Rights Act 1998 means that Britain has brought itself into line with its European counterparts. One way that rights are promoted is when complaints are made to a court and are upheld. Over time children's rights should be enhanced partly by this process.

(6)   CONFIDENTIALITY

Confidentiality is a major issue within child care, social care and education and this is quite rightly reflected within the NVQ framework. There are a number of pieces of legislation which pertain to confidentiality and social care.

This chapter will cover:

- Data Protection Act 1988
- Access to Medical Reports Act 1988
- Freedom of Information Act 2000
- Access to School Records
- Local Safeguarding Children Boards Guidelines
- Children Act 1989
- Children Act 2004

and associated regulations.

Data Protection Act 1998

This Act came into force on 1 March 2000. It replaced all of the Data Protection Act 1984 and the Access to Personal Files Act 1987. It also replaced most of the Access to Health Records Act 1990.

Individuals have a right of access to information about them held by social services departments, housing organisations or health professionals.

An individual has a right of access to all information held about them. Adults with a learning disability or a mental health problem have a right to see their file if they understand the nature of the request. Children can request to see their file and it has to be compiled with if they understand the nature of the request. Parents can request to see their son or daughters file and social services have a duty to respond as positively as possible.

Social services or health professionals can refuse access to all or part of a person's file for certain reasons e.g. where access to the information would be likely to cause serious harm to the physical or mental health of the data subject or another person. Withholding of information is expected to be used in exceptional circumstances only.

If a person is refused access to information they can appeal to either the courts or the Information Commissioner.

- the courts can order disclosure
- the Information Commissioner can issue an enforcement notice (effectively enforce disclosure)

Where a person has seen their file and feels that information is inaccurate in any way they may request the file to be amended. If they feel that this is not done they can go to the Information Commissioner or the courts to enforce correction of inaccurate information.

This Act also provides individuals with a right of access to personal information that relates to them that is held by commercial organisations on computer (e.g. insurance companies, etc).

There are several enforceable principles that underpin the DPA. These principles include:-

O information about a person must be obtained lawfully and fairly

O the information must only be used for the specified purpose

O information must be relevant, adequate and not excessive

O information must be accurate and kept up-to-date

O information must be kept no longer than necessary for the purposes specified

O organisations must have in place measures to ensure personal information is not unlawfully processed, lost or destroyed.

Access to Medical Reports Act 1988

O this gives individuals certain rights where there is a request for a medical report to be written by a doctor for employment or insurance purposes

O the individual has the right to see the medical report before it is sent to the organisation requesting it

O on seeing the report the individual may request that amendments are made

O if the doctor refuses to make the amendments then the individual can request that a statement is attached to the report outlining their own views before it is sent to the organisation that requested the report

Freedom of Information Act 2000

Direct care staff, support workers and professionals in regular contact with children and families should not get confused by the implementation of this Act.

The Freedom of Information Act 2000 gives ordinary people the right to request information from public authorities (local authorities, police, NHS organisations) about statistics and about decision making and policy making.

Information about specific individuals, such as service users or patients, remains confidential and can only be accessed by the service user themselves in line with the Data Protection Act 1998.

School Records

Guidance from the Department for Education and Skills titled Pupil Records and Reports issued in March 2000 outlines rights of access to school records.

- parents have a general right to see their child's educational records so long as their son or daughter is aged under 18

- a pupil's right to see their own school record is no longer dependant on their age. A child who submits a written request to see their school record should be allowed to do so unless it is obvious that they do not understand what they are asking for

Information will be withheld if it would be likely to cause serious harm to the physical or mental health of the pupil or that of anyone else.

Other legislation and regulations, whilst not exclusively about issues of confidentiality and access to files are relevant to this area:-

Local Safeguarding Children Boards Guidelines

These lay out guidance under which local authorities, local agencies, (schools, police, youth clubs etc) and the general public may work together to protect children from abuse. General guidance on confidentiality states that confidentiality should be broken if failing to do so would endanger a minor.

Children Act 1989 and Children Act 2004

If an investigating authority (usually social services) has reason to believe a child may suffer "significant harm", it is the duty of other agencies, for example, health, education, housing to assist by providing information and advice. Certain interpretations of the legislation would include voluntary agencies.

The Children Act 2004 Information Database (England) Regulations 2007

These place a requirement on local authorities to help operate the Contact Point database. Contact Point is a database which holds basic identifying information on every child up to the age of 18. For care leavers or young people with learning disabilities, this can be extended to 25 with their consent. Its purpose is to enable the different agencies and professionals working with children to co-ordinate their efforts and so avoid overlaps or gaps in service provision. This would meet various objectives of the Every Child Matters programme.

The regulations also cover the way in which the database will work, from creating it to accessing it. These regulations are a Statutory Instrument, ref 2007 No 2182 and can be found using a simple internet search on the title.

In Summary

It is important to be aware of the legislation which is relevant in this area, not only to ensure that you are acting within the law but also to help you to advise people on their rights in terms of access to files.

Access to files is also a spur to good practice. Anything recorded should be relevant, factual and balanced. The person you are writing about may read their file next week.

7 **HEALTH AND SAFETY**

Issues of health and safety are vital in every work role. In terms of legislation, health and safety is generally covered by statutory regulations. Perhaps this is because regulations are more easily changed than Acts of Parliament and health and safety issues need to be kept under constant review.

This chapter will cover:

- Food Safety Act 1990
- Environmental Protection Act 1990
- Activity Centres (Young People) Act 1995
- Corporate Manslaughter and Corporate Homicide Act 2007

and associated regulations.

Health and Safety at Work Act 1974

This Act outlines a number of responsibilities for employers, managers and employees.

Employers have a duty to:-

O   ensure the health and safety at work for all employees

O   provide and maintain equipment and systems which are safe and not a risk to employees' health in terms of use, handling, storage and transport of articles and substances

O   provide information, training and supervision relating to health and safety at work

Managers have a duty to:-

O   maintain a safe working environment for all staff

O   ensure that all staff adhere to policies, procedures and instructions

O   provide training for staff practices and work methods

O   explain hazards and safe working practices to new employees before they start work

O   report/record all accidents

Employees have a duty to:-

O   adhere to instructions relating to the operation of a site and equipment

O   ensure that they use materials in line with recommended procedures

O   utilise protective clothing and equipment as directed

O   not to misuse anything provided for health, safety and welfare

Associated Regulations

There are a range of regulations in the health and safety area. To aid compliance, the Health and Safety Executive (HSE) implement new regulations on only two dates per year. These are:

- 6th April
- 1st October

It is hoped that this will enable organisations to foresee change and plan for it.

The HSE publish an excellent (and brief) overview of current legislation – Health and Safety Regulation: a short guide. This can be downloaded from the HSE website at www.hse.gov.uk.

Safety Representatives and Safety Committees Regulations

If an employer recognises a trade union and that union has either appointed or is about to appoint safety representatives then the employer must consult those representatives on matters which will affect the employees they represent.

The roles of trade union safety representatives appointed under this Act are:-

- to investigate possible dangers at work, the causes of accidents and general complaints by employees on health and safety and welfare issues and to take these matters up with the employer
- to carry out inspections of the workplace particularly following accidents, diseases or other events
- to represent employees in discussions with health and safety inspectors and to receive information from those inspectors
- to attend meetings of safety committees

An employer must set up a safety committee if two or more trade union representatives ask for one.

Health and Safety (First Aid) Regulations

These regulations require employers to provide adequate equipment, facilities and personnel to enable first aid to be given to employees if they become ill or are injured at work.

The regulations do not oblige employers to provide first aid for members of the public, though the Health and Safety Executive strongly recommends that employers make provision for them.

Workplace (Health, Safety and Welfare) Regulations

These regulations complement the Management of Health and Safety at Work Regulations, and cover the management of workplaces. Duties are placed on both employers and employees (in the sense that both have control over a workplace). The main requirements created by these regulations are:-

O   the workplace, equipment, systems etc must be maintained in an efficient state

O   enclosed workplaces must be ventilated by a sufficient quantity of fresh and purified air

O   a reasonable temperature must be maintained inside buildings and a sufficient number of thermometers must be provided

O   lighting must be suitable and efficient

O   workplaces must be kept sufficiently clean

Manual Handling Operations Regulations

These cover what is often referred to as "moving and handling". The regulations contain the following main requirements:-

O   suitable and efficient assessment of all moving and handling should be made, if the handling cannot be avoided

O   risk reduction strategies must be considered by employers to reduce the risk of injury to the lowest level reasonably practicable

O   employers must provide reasonable information about

O   moving and handling

O   employers must review assessments where there is reason to suspect that circumstances have changed, and then make any necessary changes

O   employees must make full and proper use of any system of work provided by the employer

Reporting of Injuries, Diseases and Dangerous Occurrences Regulations

These regulations are often referred to as RIDDOR. The regulations require the reporting of work-related accidents, diseases and dangerous occurrences. Employers, self employed people and people in control of work premises have duties under the regulations to report:

O deaths or major injuries at work

O work related injuries which result in people being away from work for over 3 days

O work related diseases

O dangerous occurrences at work

Health and Safety (Consultation with Employees) Regulations

Any employees not in groups covered by trade union Safety Representatives must be consulted by their employers under these regulations. An employer can choose to consult them directly or through elected representatives.

Elected representatives of employees have the following roles:-

O to take up with employers concerns about possible risks and dangerous events in the workplace that may affect the employees they represent

O to take up with employers general matters affecting the health and safety of the employees they represent

O to represent the employees who elected them in consultations with Health and Safety inspectors

Employers may choose to give elected representatives extra roles.

Road Vehicles (Construction and Use) Regulations

These regulations require minibuses and coaches used to transport children to have seat belts.

Management of Health and Safety at Work Regulations

These state that employers have to provide training for staff:-

O when they start work

O when their work or responsibilities change and there are new or greater risks o periodically if needed - for instance if the skills do not get used regularly

The training must be during working hours and not at the expense of employees.

Education (School Premises) Regulations

These regulations set standards for school premises. These include requirements for the structure of buildings and for fire safety. There is a general requirement that the health and safety of the people in a school building or on school land must be "reasonably assured." Under Section 542 of the Education Act 1996 the Local Education Authority must ensure that schools meet the standards set by these regulations.

In addition to the Health and Safety at Work Act 1974 and the Regulations covered there are other Acts of Parliament which relate to other aspects of health and safety.

Control of Substances Hazardous to Health Regulations

These regulations are often referred to as COSHH.

The regulations cover substances which can cause ill health. Any substances such as cleaning materials, waste products, fumes etc are covered.

In order to comply with the regulations employers must:-

o assess the risks to health arising from work
o decide what precautions are needed
o prevent or control exposure to substances hazardous to health
o ensure that control measures are used and maintained
o monitor exposure of workers to hazardous substances and where assessment shows that health surveillance may be needed to carry out such surveillance
o ensure that employees are properly informed, trained and supervised

Regulatory Reform (Fire Safety) Order 2005

This Statutory Instrument reforms the fire safety regulations that apply to England and Wales.

In any workplace the employer has a responsibility to:

- take fire precautions to ensure, as far as possible, the safety of all employees
- to ensure there are general fire precautions to keep the property safe (and so protect the general public) (article 8)

The employers duties include:

- carry out a risk assessment to identify the general fire precautions that are needed and then (article 9)
- apply any fire prevention measure and have in place an evacuation procedure (articles 10 to 18)
- inform employees of the risks and the fire prevention measures (articles 19 to 21)

Employees have duties which include (article 23)

- follow all fire safety requirements as directed by their employer
- inform the employer of any risks not adequately addressed

Product Liability

Product liability is established under Part 1 of the Consumer Protection Act 1987. Product liability means that under the Consumer Protection Act 1987 a manufacturer is liable for injury caused, or property that is damaged, due to faulty equipment that they have provided. The manufacturer is also responsible for providing information about the safe use of the equipment. Hence instructions are often stuck to equipment as well as being provided in leaflets or booklets. Product liability could apply equally to hoists, other aids and adaptations as well as an office chair.

If the equipment is not faulty and is used satisfactorily then liability for it's safe use transfers to the employer.

Provision and Use of Work Equipment Regulations (PUWER)

These Regulations impose a range of duties on employers (and to a limited extent to the employees who use the equipment). Aspects include:

O The initial state of the equipment
O Use of equipment for the proper purpose
O Suitability of equipment
O Maintenance
O Inspection
O Training staff in it's use

The scope of these Regulations has been interpreted very broadly so that is includes cupboards and curtain rails as well as equipment that is subject to heavy usage. The employer's liability is strictly applied. Even if the equipment was regularly inspected and then it unexpectedly fell and injured a staff member the employer is still liable. The employer would not be liable for negligence if the equipment was satisfactorily maintained and inspected, but they would still be liable for any injury under these Regulations.

Lifting Operations and Lifting Equipment Regulations

These Regulations apply to lifting equipment used at work. Lifting equipment would include hoists, stairlifts and through floor lifts. The Regulations impose a range of duties on employers and to a limited extent on staff who use or supervise the use of the equipment. Duties include:

O Ensuring adequate strength and stability
O Positioning and installation
O Marking of safe working loads
O Organisation of lifting operations
O Examination and inspection
O Reporting defects, and acting on these reports

There is no set guidance as to how frequently lifting equipment should be inspected. This is partly dependent on whether the equipment is exposed to conditions that could cause it to deteriorate such that dangerous situations could arise. Some hoist manufacturers recommend a thorough examination of their hoists every six months. Against this the Health and Safety Executive have published a document recommending that hoists are inspected at least every twelve months. The implication is that some manufacturers could have a conflict of interests. (That is they can charge a care organisation every time their trained inspectors go out on a visit.) What is clear is that the time scales for thorough inspections should be drawn up by a competent person who is aware of all relevant facts.

Food Safety Act 1990

This Act applies wherever food is supplied other than within a family situation. Therefore, all settings which involve the supply of food must comply with hygiene and other food safety requirements.

This Act is a wide ranging piece of legislation which strengthened and updated existing laws relevant to food safety.

The Act sets out a number of requirements about food produced for human consumption:-

O   food provided must not be injurious to health
O   it must not be unfit to eat
O   it must not be contaminated

The Food Safety Act and all food legislation is enforced through environmental health officers and trading standards officers who are employed by local authorities.

Food Hygiene (England) Regulations

These new food hygiene regulations came into force in 2006 and bring together recent European legislation and update the Food Safety Act 1990.

They are said to present a new "flexible" approach to food hygiene practice whilst optimising public health and setting in place new responsibilities and penalties. Of the many requirements it contains, one stands out in the context of this book:

"All operators of food businesses must register with their Local Authority Environmental Health Department and that includes kitchens of care establishments and public sector organisations."

The kitchen manager is responsible for responding to these regulations and ensuring staff are aware of them too. The HSE document "Food Law Code of Practice" makes specific mention of the need to particularly safeguard people who are deemed vulnerable from poor hygiene practice. For such critical legislation, it is important to get the whole story. The Food Law Code of Practice document entitled "Safer Food, Better Business" can be obtained free from the HSE or by telephoning: 0845 606 0667.

Environmental Protection Act 1990

This is a very wide ranging piece of legislation, much of which is probably not relevant to social care staff. Some sections, however, may have a direct bearing on your work. For example, section 34 of the Act places a duty of care on anyone who *"produces, imports, carries, keeps, treats or disposes of household, commercial, or industrial "* waste.

In addition, the Environmental Protection Act contains the main legislation for England and Wales on statutory nuisance. A variety of definitions of statutory nuisance are outlined within the Act. However, those which may be most relevant are:-

O any premises in such a state as to be prejudicial to health or a nuisance

O noise emitted from premises so as to be prejudicial to health or a nuisance

Activity Centres (Young People) Act 1995

This Act allows the Health and Safety Commission to make regulations for children's activity centres and the people who provide them. Such centres might be for sport or outdoor pursuits. The Act also makes provision for the licensing of such facilities and the collection of fees and the enforcement of its own regulations. It does not, in itself contain any standards and the Health and Safety Commission should be contacted for these.

Corporate Manslaughter and Corporate Homicide Act 2007

This Act received Royal Assent on 26th July 2007. It amends case law and generally the Law of Negligence

Most of this Act came into force on 6th April 2008 and it basically does just one thing; it creates a new offence of Corporate Manslaughter, or in Scotland, Corporate Homicide. The differing terminology is simply in order to fit with existing legal structures on each side of the border. The Act is, aside from this, UK wide legislation.

The offence of Corporate Manslaughter/Homicide is not new however, but has always been wrapped up in a mass of case law and other legislation known collectively as the Law of Negligence. In the old system, a company could only be convicted if one high up individual, known legally as a "controlling mind" could be seen as almost personally culpable for the death of a person through the company's activities. Years of accident investigations have shown that fatal incidents, and indeed corporations, do not work like that. There is usually a string of events that lead to an incident.
The new Act therefore redefines the offence and the causes required to be present for a case of Corporate manslaughter/homicide to be brought. It happens like this:

O   A death occurs. Obvious really, but if someone is "only" severely injured, standard health and safety legislation still applies.

O   The death does not have to be an employee of the company concerned but it does have to result from the way that company's activities were managed or organised.

O   Also, the death must have arisen from a gross breach of the company's duty of care to the victim.

O   Lastly, the organisational failings that led to the death must have been somehow authorised by senior management. That is to say, practices that were authored or agreed to or known about by senior management. Senior management does not just include Directors either.

Please also note that this Act does not introduce any new duties on organisations but does, interestingly, extend to organisations engaged in illegal activities. The Act applies to any business in the UK or foreign businesses operating in the UK from partnerships upwards. Single traders are not covered. Crown Bodies and government organisations are covered including the Prison Service and the Army.

In order that certain people doing dangerous jobs can get on and do them without their employers being paralysed by legislation there are certain exemptions, where charges under this Act may not be brought. Some are "comprehensive", for example soldiers in battle and training, while others are "partial" which is where some aspects of social care come in.

Partial Exemptions

While social work and probation departments are still covered by this Act in their duties as employers and occupiers of buildings; they are exempt from prosecution under this Act when their staff are carrying out statutory inspection functions and other frontline aspects of their jobs. It is difficult to see how this will work in practice and it will be shaped by case law but if, for example, a social worker visits a house to investigate a claim of abuse and is killed by a client then, provided their employer had not failed in their duties as an employer, no charge can be brought against the employer under this Act. Other occupations subject to partial exemptions include lifeboat crews and mountain rescue teams which rather puts the job into perspective doesn't it?

 In Summary

We all have responsibilities in terms of health and safety at work. It is important to be aware of these responsibilities and to have at least a basic understanding of the law which informs this area of practice.

It should be noted that Health and Safety legislation changes slowly and with good reason. People need to be able to keep up with it and have knowledge of it, so there cannot be sweeping changes very often. What changes there are tend to react to specific developments in technology or new risks such as chemical or biological hazards.

8   CHILDREN AT WORK

Sandwiched between the chapters on health and safety and protecting children, this chapter sits comfortably in both of these areas! This is a tricky and complex area and this chapter seeks to provide a concise overview of the legislation covering children at work.

This chapter will cover:

- Children and Young Persons Act 1933
- Children and Young Persons Act 1963
- Children Act 1972
- Merchant Shipping Act 1995
- Education Act 1996

and associated regulations.

The Children and Young Persons Act 1933

This area is often the subject for much debate and it is principally regulated by the Children and Young Persons Act 1933 with many subsequent additions and regulations. Essentially, children under the age of 14 cannot be employed. Exceptions are governed by local by-laws and the child is granted a licence by the local authority. Subject to local authority approval, 13 year olds can take part in paid performances and modelling or be licenced to work for their parents. Traditionally, this was in light agricultural work so consulting your local authority is essential if the child is under 14. Anecdotal evidence, however, suggests that the local authority licencing system has failed into disuse in some areas.

Working 14 year olds

Once a child reaches 14 years old, a whole world of employment opportunities opens up for them, with certain restrictions and conditions. These are:

o   Work shall only be what the 1933 Act calls "light work", therefore it will not risk their health, nor will it interfere with their education
o   During school holidays it will not exceed 5 hours per day, Monday to Saturday and only 2 hours on Sundays
o   They shall not work during school hours, nor before 7am or after 7pm with a maximum of 2 hours per day on school days
o   A maximum of 12 hours work per week during the school term and
o   25 hours maximum per week during the school holidays
o   In any case, no more than 4 hours work without a break
o   14 year olds must get at least two consecutive weeks per year when they do not work. (These cannot be school weeks.)

They are not allowed to do:

o   Street trading (some local authorities will licence this if it is for their parents.)
o   Performances abroad – unless a licence is issued by a Justice of the Peace
o   Scrap metal selling
o   Work in a betting shop or petrol station
o   House to house charity collections

15 to 16 year olds

This age group has largely the same list of restrictions as 14 year olds. However, there is an increase in the number of hours they can work. Outside of the school term, they may now work 8 hours on weekdays and Saturdays to a maximum of 35 hours per week.

Children and Young Persons Act 1963

Part II of this Act specifies the times that a minor may be absent from school for the performance of paid entertainments, and the issuing of a license from the local authority for under 16s doing so.

Children Act 1972

This Act ensures that changes in the school leaving age, do not affect the laid down minimum ages at which children may work, thus making education and employment two separate issues, not necessarily one following the other. This may be useful in the implementation of work experience schemes and on the job training etc.

The Act also specifies that notwithstanding changes in the school leaving age, the minimum age at which a child can work in any paid setting is 13. Please note that this is a minimum age. Local by-laws can require a child to be older before being allowed to work.

Prevention of Accidents to Children in Agriculture Regulations 1994

This is a Statutory Instrument of the 1974 Health and Safety at Work Act. This means that it is a set of legally binding regulations which were added to the original legislation after it was written. The regulations define a child as under 13, but this is only for these regulations. They go onto prohibit a 'child' from riding on or driving a tractor or riding on trailers or associated machinery.

Merchant Shipping Act 1995

This Act prohibits children working on board ships.

Education Act 1996

The work related legislation in this Act is for children under compulsory school age (section 558-559). This Act avoids naming specific ages and instead gives powers to a local education authority to prohibit any employer from employing a specific child if s/he is being employed in such a manner as to be "prejudicial to health, or otherwise to render him unfit to obtain the full benefit of the education provided for him." That authority may give notice to that employer in writing and if the child continues to be employed then the employer is guilty of an offence. The LEA may also ask for information about the employment which must also be supplied to avoid the employer or parent committing an offence. This approach allows for a greater assessment of the child's needs rather than purely relating to ages. Of course, other legislation which does quote ages still remains in force and should not be ignored. Work experience is regulated separately in the next section of this Act.

Health and Safety at Work Regulations 1999 (SI 1999 No. 19)

This statutory instrument builds upon the 1933 Act and makes a number of points about what types of work cannot be given to people under the age of 18.

Under 18s

- Cannot be given work which is beyond their physical and psychological capacity
- Cannot be exposed to radiation or other potentially harmful toxins
- Cannot be put in a situation that carries risks that, because of their young age, they might not be able to anticipate
- Cannot be exposed to extremes of heat, cold, noise or vibration
- Exceptions to the above can include training situations or under strict supervision or where risks have been removed as far as can be reasonably anticipated.

Children (Protection At Work) Regulations 2000

Another Statutory Instrument, this time from the Children and Young Persons Act 1933. These slightly amend the older Act and achieve the following:

O raise to 13 years the minimum age at which local authority bylaws may allow children to be employed in light agricultural or horticultural work

O local regulations allowing children to take part in street trading must state the number of hours and days they are allowed to do so

O only 16 year olds over the school leaving age may take part in dangerous performances. For example some circus acts and so forth

These minor modifications to a fairly old Act are really there to bring it into line with other, more recent legislation such as the 1996 Education Act.

In Summary

Children at work could fit into a number of the chapters of this book. This is an issue relating to rights, health and safety and protecting children. It is an area which all staff working with older children and young people need to be aware of. As with the other chapters of this book, remember, we are only providing an overview. If this is an area which is important in your work role, ensure you see the full detail of the legislation referred to.

(9) PROTECTING CHILDREN

The legislation covering the protection of children from abuse is mainly found in the Children Act 1989. For example sections 1 (welfare principle), 17 (children in need, significant harm etc), Part IV (Protection of Children). However, the procedures, duties of local authorities and responsibilities of other agencies are located in the Children Act 2004. One key agency in England and Wales is the Local Safeguarding Children's Board (LSCB) which must have senior managers from local authorities, health and the police working to safeguard children.

Additionally local agencies in England and Wales follow guidance such as "Working Together to Safeguard Children" which is updated or added to whenever necessary. The accepted method for interviewing children, particularly using video, who may have been physically or sexually abused, is laid out in guidance issued by the Home Office. This is a complex and increasingly specialised area, often dealt with by dedicated Child Protection teams. Whilst being aware of the relevant legislation, staff should also be aware of local procedures. There is never any justification for carrying out your own investigation. Doing so will often weaken any case in court and could put a child or young person through the trauma of having to explain what has happened more times than is necessary.

Every relevant agency, school, children's home etc should have a copy of the local LSCB guidelines in its shelves. For a full awareness of this subject, staff should familiarise themselves with it. In Wales, agencies should have a copy of the All Wales Child Protection Procedures.

This chapter will cover, in brief, some of the key legislation covering this area. However, as stated, this is a complex and increasingly specialised area. The information given in this chapter is for quick reference only. Refer to the relevant law for more information.

Children Act 1989

This Act lays out the conditions and, indeed, duties by which the state can and should interrupt the privacy of family life and parental responsibility in order to protect children. The report into the death of Jasmine Beckford, or the Cleveland enquiry show the two extremes of under and over involvement by the state. In this chapter, we are concerned with two aspects which are: duties to protect under the Children Act 1989 and orders which the Court can make under the Act to protect children. It is a central principle of the Act however, that no order should be made if duties can be carried out with only a lesser order or no order at all (the No/Lesser Order Principle).

Section 47 of the Act states the local authority's duty to investigate where it has reasonable cause to suspect that a child may suffer 'significant harm'. Such enquiries should consider what action may be needed to safeguard that child's welfare, and this may involve removing the child under the orders discussed below.

Police Protection, (s.46), maximum 72 hours. Incorrectly called a Police Protection Order. A constable can remove a child to a safe place if s/he has reason to believe that there is risk of 'significant harm'. The process must then be handed to the local authority as soon as possible and reasonable parental access to the child cannot be denied if in the child's best interests.

Child Assessment Order (s.43): can be made if there is no other way, for example by parental agreement, for the local authority to assess the risk a child is under. Lasting seven days, it places the parent or guardian under a legal obligation to produce the child and allow such investigations as are necessary to determine long or short term risk.

Emergency Protection Orders: Not to exceed eight days. This allows removal of a child if there is reason to believe there is a risk of significant harm to a child. Through amendments introduced by Schedule 6 of the Family Law Act 1996, the Emergency Protection Order can specify a person who is excluded from the child's home.

Care Order (s.31): This Order ultimately gives the local authority full parental responsibility and the right to decide how much parental responsibility may be exercised by the parents. This can only be made where the parents will not co-operate with the local authority in its duties to investigate or protect a child. An Interim Care Order can be made if court procedures are likely to cause delay

Section 8 Orders: These are a range of orders that a court can make, both on behalf of the local authority and others (such as family members). They are: Contact Orders, Prohibited Steps Order, residence Order, Specific Issues Order. Please refer to the Act for further details.

Children and Young Persons (Harmful Publications) Act 1955

This Act makes it an offence to distribute printed material, mainly pictorial, which "would tend to corrupt" a child or young person who might get access to it. The Act specifically mentions material which portrays:

- the commission of crimes, or
- acts of violence or cruelty, or
- incidents of a repulsive or horrible nature

Child Abduction and Custody Act 1985

This Act ratified, that is signed the United Kingdom up to, two international conventions: the Hague Convention and the European Convention. This means that all states which are members of one or both of these conventions will co-operate with one another to recover a child who has been abducted from one member state to another if the abduction is against a custody decision made in the country where the child was abducted.

Sexual Offences Act 2003

Adults who work with young people in care or educational services are in a position of trust. If an adult worker enters into a sexual relationship, or behaves in sexual ways with a 16 or 17 year old child who is resident at that care service or attends that service (eg: educational institution), then this is an offence. Sections 16-19 of the Sexual Offences Act 2003 detail the different sexual activities that are prohibited, and the range of staff who are included (this range is intentionally broad).

Organisational Aspects of Protecting Children

Protection of Children Act 1999

This is an Act which requires that a list be kept of persons who are considered as unsuitable to be allowed to work with children.

The 1999 Act covers these areas:

The Secretary of State has a duty to keep a list as described above. A "Child Care Organisation" shall refer an individual to the Secretary of State for a variety of reasons. Some will seem obvious, such as misconduct which placed a child at risk, but it also includes:

where an individual has resigned before they could be dismissed for such misconduct or has been transferred to a role within the organisation which has no contact with children, because of such misconduct.

The Secretary of State may, at any time, remove an individual from the list if s/he is satisfied that they should not be included on it.

The Act specifies the grounds under which an agency shall refer and how the decision for inclusion on the list is made. Appeals procedures are also covered.

Education legislation is further modified under this Act to afford greater protection to children in education, particularly those with special needs, which is an intention of the Act.

The Act specifies that any child care agency which intends to offer employment to an individual shall consult both this list and the Department for Education and Skills list and shall not offer employment if the individual appears on either of them. Employment agencies may offer staff whom they have so checked in the last twelve months.

The Police Act 1997 is modified to include checks on these lists when "Police Checks" are requested by child care agencies.

Children Act 2004

English Local Authorities

All statutory services that provide services to children have a duty to ensure that in carrying out their functions they have regard to the need to safeguard and promote the welfare of children. This duty applies even where the statutory agency (eg a local authority) contracts out services for children (s.11).

All statutory agencies that work with children have a duty to co-operate with the local authority in order to improve the wellbeing of children in their area, while the local authority has a duty to co-ordinate local arrangements (s.10).

Each local authority must establish a Local Safeguarding Children Board (LSCB). The composition of LSCB's is detailed by regulations issued by the Secretary of State (DfES).

Welsh Local Authorities

A duty is placed on local authorities to improve the well being of children in their area and to do this by co-operating with partner agencies. The partner agencies have a duty placed on them to co-operate with the local authority (s.25).

The local authority and all partner agencies referred to in the 2004 Act must carry out their duties in a manner that safeguards and promotes the welfare of children (s.28).

Local authorities are required to take the lead in establishing Local Safeguarding Children's Boards (LSCB). Guidance on how the LSCBs will operate will be issued by the Assembly (s.31-34).

The Local Children Safeguarding Boards Regulations 2006
Ref: 2006 No. 90 England
Ref: 2006 No. 1705 Wales

These regulations state that local authorities in England and Wales are required to establish Local Safeguarding Children Boards (LSCBs) in their area. They are made up of local authority representatives and relevant partner agencies such as Police and NHS bodies.

These regulations set out the functions of the boards and also who should be involved with them and how they work procedurally.

Importantly, LCSBs replaced Area Child Protection Committees and introduced a new statutory requirement for the above mentioned partner agencies to be involved. LCSBs also contribute to the local Children and Young People's Plan.

From 1st April 2008 they will also collect and analyse data on local child deaths in order to inform both preventative and reactive policy and practice.

As always, further ready of the actual regulations is recommended.

Safeguarding Vulnerable Groups Act 2006

This Act received Royal Assent on 8th November 2006. It amends the Children Act 1989, Teaching and Higher Education Act 1998, Protection of Children Act 1999, Care Standards Act 2000, Childcare Act 2006, Data Protection Act 1998, Adoption and Children Act 2002, among others.

In essence this Act is a major revision, and streamlining of the system for vetting people who work with children and vulnerable adults. It resulted from the Bichard Inquiry Report, published in June 2004. The previous system had been fragmented and only truly accurate on the date checks were first carried out. One aim of the new scheme is to make it proactive rather than reactive. The Act, and therefore the new scheme, applies across England and Wales with the scheme having close ties with Scotland.

The Act provides a legislative framework for a new vetting and barring scheme for people working with children or vulnerable adults. It classifies various paid and unpaid activities covered by the scheme and institutes a barring system to stop undesirable individuals from working in these occupations.

The Act sets up the Independent Barring Board (IBB) which maintains two lists; one for work with children and one for work with adults. The IBB also makes decisions about who goes on these lists. Under the scheme, there are four routes to inclusion on either or both lists:

O Automatic inclusion for receiving a caution or conviction for certain specified offences or other criteria such as inclusion on a foreign list with no right of appeal.

O Automatic inclusion for receiving a caution or conviction for certain specified offences but with the right of appeal.

O Specified Behaviours, called "relevant conduct" in the Act, which includes conduct which harms a child or vulnerable adult or conduct involving, for example, child pornography.

O Risk of Harm – this is where evidence suggests that an individual may present a risk of harm to children or vulnerable adults.

These last two do not lead to automatic inclusion but are subject to consideration by the IBB for inclusion on the appropriate list. It should be noted that these last two do not require a conviction. This blocks a loophole in the system where, for example, a community "knows" that a person presents a risk and police have genuine concerns but a conviction has not been possible. People included on these lists may not engage in "regulated" or "controlled" activities involving children or vulnerable adults and the Act creates various requirements and offences to ensure that they do not.

Domestic Violence

The links between domestic violence and harm to children have been well established for some time now (see for example Hughes et al 1989). The Home Office and Department of Health have published various policy documents outlining the importance of tackling violence against women. See for example Domestic Violence: Break the Chain. Multi-Agency Guidance for Addressing Domestic Violence (Home Office 2000).

There are a number of Acts that are relevant when considering how to respond to domestic violence or abuse.

Children Act 1989

The Children Act 1989 has been amended to reflect the seriousness of domestic violence.

When a court is considering applications under Section 8 and it is also considering whether a child has suffered or is likely to suffer harm, it must consider harm that a child may suffer from witnessing domestic violence. (This amendment was introduced through the Adoption and Children Act 2002.)

Emergency Protection Orders and Interim Care Orders can have an exclusion order with powers of arrest attached to remove a suspected child abuser from the home. Certain criteria have to be met for such an exclusion order to be granted by a court.

Family Law Act 1996

Part IV of this Act relates to protecting a vulnerable person from domestic abuse. The civil court actions that a person can take to protect themselves consists of applying for

- a non-molestation order. A court can require a person who has been 'associated' with the victim to stop engaging in violent, threatening or pestering behaviour.

- occupation order. A person who has been 'associated' with an individual, such that they shared a common home either as a married couple or cohabiting partners, can apply for a occupation order in respect of the shared home. The court can make an occupation order if certain conditions are satisfied these include that the applicant is likely to suffer harm due to the behaviour of their partner (or ex-partner) if the order is not made. Powers of arrest can also be attached to the order.

The Family Law Act 1996 has been strengthened by the Domestic Violence, Crime and Victims Act 2004. Sections inserted into the Family Law Act 1996 make breaching a non-molestation order an arrestable offence.

Additionally occupancy orders were originally only available in situations involving heterosexual couples. This has also been amended so an individual in a same sex relationship can now obtain an occupancy order.

Protection from Harassment Act 1997

A person who is subjected to harassment or intimidatory pestering can seek protection through both the criminal and civil courts.

Domestic Violence, Crime and Victims Act 2004

This Act inserts new stronger sections into both the Family Law Act 1996 and the Protection from Harassment Act 1997.

The Mental Health Act 2007 amended this Act to provide new rights for victims of offenders who have a mental disorder but aren't subject to any restrictions. Victims can make representations to receive information about discharge dates, treatment and conditions. There is also a framework for victims to have input into the decision making process when conditions are being decided.

Housing Act 1996

This Act imposes on local authorities a duty to house people who are unintentionally homeless and in priority need.

Individuals who are homeless as a result of domestic abuse should be eligible for accommodation.

Criminal Law

Anyone who is subjected to domestic violence has the same rights to seek protection from the police and the criminal justice system as anyone else who is subjected to similar violence committed against them by a complete stranger.

In Summary

Everyone has responsibilities in terms of child protection. It is important that you are aware of your responsibilities and that you have a basic understanding of the legal framework of child protection. You should also understand your Local Safeguarding Childrens Board guidelines.

(10) LOOKED AFTER CHILDREN

The term 'Looked After' replaces the term 'in care' and generally refers to any child, whether on a Care Order or not, who is residing in some form of substitute care which is overseen by the local authority. The use of terms like 'in care', 'looked after' etc vary in their usage from local authority to local authority so it is always worth asking if the child is on a Care Order or not. Some children live in certain special educational or health establishments. This is not, in itself equivalent to being 'in care' or 'Looked After' for the purposes of this chapter. However the local authority does have certain duties to monitor children's well-being in these establishments. The principal body of legislation for Looked After Children is the Children Act 1989.

Children Act 1989

O the term 'Accommodated' usually refers to children provided with accommodation under section 20 of the Act. This is the old 'voluntary care' used to assist families rather than provide protection to a child. An example would be a parent staying in hospital or falling ill, or a temporary arrangement due to high levels of family stress. Under such arrangements, parental responsibility remains with the parents, with certain aspect such as administering emergency medical treatment, being temporarily delegated to the local authority, usually by written consent

O Care Order (s.31), is a Court Order which gives the local authority greater parental responsibility, and therefore control, than the parent

O respite care. Given under section 20 but for very short, often regular periods, perhaps to relieve parents caring for a child with a disability

O it is the responsibility of the local authority to review all such arrangements at least every six months by the use of planning meetings and reviews. These are chaired by an Independent Chairperson following a prescribed format which focuses on the young person's needs, wishes and feelings. Any involved person including the child can call a review at any time

O section 17 states a local authority's duty to avoid reception into the "Looked After System" or to avoid significant harm whenever possible through the giving of help, advice and in exceptional circumstances, cash

O also included in the "Looked After System" is the facility for restricting the liberty of a young person in certain circumstances

Arrangements for Placement of Children (General) Regulations 1991

These regulations are a Statutory Instrument of the Children Act. This means that they are an extension of the Act, issued after it was passed. They are therefore to be treated as legislation. These regulations are very much within the spirit of the rest of the Children Act 1989, making strong links to its basic principles (e.g. the Welfare Principle). They give detail to the following areas of work:

O   making arrangements to place children and maintain their
    welfare

O   issues to consider when making such placements

O   arrangements for contact for children placed in voluntary
    organisations and registered children's homes

O   record keeping and confidentiality and access by Guardians ad
    Litem (people nominated by the Court to independently examine
    arrangements)

O   arrangements across local authority boundaries

Please refer to the actual Regulations for more information. This is a
general overview only.

Placement of Children with Parents etc Regulations 1991

This Statutory Instrument to the Children Act lays out the procedures
and considerations which a local authority must undertake if they
intend to place children who are under a Care Order with a parent or
parents of that child. This may seem like a contradiction, and it is a
strange situation for all concerned. This child would live with a parent
but with the Care Order in place. The local authority would still have
an ultimate say as to the care of that child. It is however, wholly in
accordance with the principles of the Children Act which place a duty
on local authorities to attempt to maintain children in their own homes
and families.

These procedures constitute an approval process which in many
ways mirrors the processes applied to foster carers or adopters. The
ultimate approval, following the preparation of a report, lies with the
Director of Children's Services or by a specifically nominated officer.
If the child is over 16, however, many of the prescribed checks do not
apply because the child is seen to be of an age and understanding
where s/he can be part of this decision process. Relevant local
agencies and significant people must be notified of any decision to
place under these regulations and the placement shall thereafter be
monitored and supported by the local authority. It is essential that
persons involved in such a placement or assessment consult the
actual regulations as these notes are for general information only.

Children and Young Person's Bill 2007-2008
Territorial Extent: England and Wales

In June 2007, the Government published the White Paper "Care Matters: Time for Change." Essentially, its aim is to improve the outcomes for children and young people in and leaving care. The poor outcomes and life chances of children and young people and adults who have been in care are very well documented.

This bill aims to reform the statutory framework of the looked after system. The changes are wide ranging, yet appear to target much of what has failed looked after children and young people since the 1989 Children Act.

By way of a summary, the new Bill proposals are:

o Local authorities may use private provision to provide social work services, regulated under the Care Standards Act 2000. However, in the case of children's residential services, they can also issue compliance notices to improve or suspend admissions if appropriate, so a good deal of control is retained.

o Greater protection for looked after children against their being moved from their local school or area of residence.

o Enhanced role for Independent Reviewing Officers

o Explicit and enhanced duties on local authorities to provide independent visitors/befrienders/advisers to looked after children and young people. This is now extended to those in youth custody and residential placements

o Governors of maintained schools to appoint a member of staff to promote the achievements of looked after pupils

o For care leavers, an extended duty on local authorities to provide personal advisers, assisting pathway plans and engagement in further education and training

o Local authority bursaries for care leavers in higher education

o New powers for local authorities to make cash payments to children in need and their families

o Amended procedures for reporting child deaths to local safeguarding children boards

- Brings the checks on independent fostering reviews more into line with adoption processes

- Relatives who may apply for a residence order, without leave of the court, now to include those with whom the child or young person has lived for one year or more

- Repeals section 45(9) of the 1989 Children Act, removing the 72 hour moratorium on courts hearing an application for the discharge of an emergency protection order

This Bill really appears to be a considered response to failing of the looked after system in recent times. This author, a cynical ex-social worker, feels that properly applied, this legislation could bring significant new safeguards for looked after children and young people.

In Summary

This chapter has given a basic overview of the concept of "looked after" children. Aspects of legislation surrounding residential care and fostering/adoption are covered in the following two chapters.

(11) RESIDENTIAL CARE

The Children Act 1989 placed a duty upon local authorities to provide 'Community Homes' to provide accommodation for children in its care and to promote the welfare of other children in its area. There must be a range of options, for example catering for different ages etc, although the authority may make such arrangements as it 'considers appropriate' leaving some room for variations in the way this duty is met from authority to authority.

The local authority therefore has to directly provide residential care itself or arrange for other care organisations to provide the necessary residential care.

It is important to bear in mind that residential care for children and young people is only one option for ensuring looked after children are cared for.

This chapter covers the Regulations applicable to residential care for Children.

Regulation and Inspection of Children's Residential Services

The regulation and inspection of children's residential services is the responsibility of the Commission for Social Care Inspection (CSCI). The CSCI is given this task by the Care Standards Act 2000 (as amended by the Health and Social Care (Community Health and Standards) Act 2003).

The Care Standards Act 2000 defines a children's home as:-

"An establishment is a children's home .... if it provides care and accommodation wholly or mainly for children" (s.1).

(Accommodation where a child lives with a parent, relative or foster carer is specifically exempted from the definition).

A school that provides residential accommodation to at least one child for more than 295 days in twelve months is also defined as a children's home (s.1).

The definition of children's home therefore includes all the different types of traditional children's homes as identified in the Children Act 1989. Hence community homes, voluntary homes and registered private children's homes are all counted as children's homes. Even if there is only one child in an establishment that service must be registered as a children's home.

All children's homes must register with the CSCI. The CSCI must inspect all children's homes and evaluate the children's home against the regulations and national minimum standards that detail standards of care in children's homes.

The Secretary of State is given the authority by the Care Standards Act 2000 to draw up and issue regulations and national minimum standards (s.22 and s.23).

The CSCI is then responsible for applying the regulations and national minimum standards.

The inspectors appointed by the CSCI are given the power to enter and inspect any care service (this clearly includes children's homes) (s.31).

The Children's Homes Regulations 2001

These replace the Children's Homes Regulations 1991. They are relatively detailed and cover all the significant aspects of the management and running of a children's home.

The Regulations make direct reference to the home having:-

O   a statement of purpose
O   a policy on safeguarding children
O   a policy on behaviour management
O   a complaints procedure

(this list is not exhaustive).

Various management issues are addressed including fitness of registered manager; levels of staffing; management of staffing and fitness of premises.

National Minimum Standards for Children's Homes

Even though the Children's Homes Regulations are fairly detailed the National Minimum Standards expand on the Regulations and make more explicit what is required.

For example the Regulations state that staff should "receive appropriate training, supervision and appraisal".

The National Minimum Standards state that each member of staff should receive one and a half hours of one to one supervision from a senior member of staff each month.

The National Minimum Standards go into far more detail of what is expected within the children's home.

Every children's home is required to have the Regulations and Standards available for anyone (children, young people, staff, relatives) connected with the service to view.

Children Accommodated in Educational and Health Establishments

The well being and safety of children who are accommodated either in health or educational establishments has been recognised as an area that needs overview for some time.

The Children Act 1989 contains several sections (85, 86 and 87) which relate to children in long term health or special education establishments or independent schools. One of the general areas of concern is that children with long term illnesses or a disability who are accommodated in health or educational establishments are at risk of isolation and all the additional risk factors associated with this.

It is a requirement of the Children Act that the proprietor of a school or the governing body of the school (where children are accommodated) must safeguard and promote the well being of all children accommodated.

The Care Standards Act 2000 amends section 87 of the Children Act 1989 so that the CSCI has a duty to apply regulations and national minimum standards that are drawn up specifically for different types of educational establishments which accommodate children.

National Care Standards Commission (Inspection of Schools and Colleges) Regulations 2002

These regulations are relatively brief and general when compared to the Children's Homes Regulations 2001. The Inspection of Schools and Colleges Regulations state that authorised individuals (inspectors) can inspect educational premises and make enquiries necessary to carry out the inspection. These Regulations apply to residential special schools and boarding schools.

National Minimum Standards for Residential Special Schools 2002

These Standards support the Inspection of Schools and Colleges Regulations. They are very detailed and cover all aspects of the care of children. They do not address educational issues, (that's for Ofsted).

National Minimum Standards for Boarding Schools 2002

These Standards support the Inspection of Schools and Colleges Regulations in respect of boarding schools.

These Standards are also detailed and relate to aspects of the boarding schools outside of teaching time.

Guidance on Permissible Forms of Control in Children's Residential Care

The guidance on this sensitive but important practice issue is currently contained in the Local Authority Circular (LAC) (93) 13. This guidance does not extend to foster care or schools (except schools that are registered children's homes).

Additionally, staff and managers should cross reference this guidance with regulation 17 of the Care Homes Regulations 2001. Regulation 17 details the need for a written behaviour management policy, the types of disciplinary measures that are unacceptable and what managers need to do following the use of any measure of control or discipline.

Staff in homes for children with learning disabilities should be aware of "Guidance for Restrictive Physical Interventions. How to Provide Safe Services for People with Learning Disabilities and Autistic Spectrum Disorder" (see below).

The guidance LAC(93)13 makes clear the importance of creating a positive child care environment. This includes seeking to support children express their concerns in acceptable ways and making clear the acceptable boundaries of behaviour and control in the service.

The guidance on the use of physical restraint - when it is acceptable to use restraint, what are the acceptable limits etc is detailed and cannot be justly conveyed in a small number of bullet points. Staff are advised to read the guidance themselves.

Following any incident involving restraint the guidance makes clear the importance of recording the incident; providing support to the child involved; discussion between the staff member involved and the manager; report to line manager etc.

It is very important that staff teams do not develop a 'bravado' culture where physical responses become routine.

Guidance for Restrictive Physical Interventions. How to Provide Safe Services for People with Learning Disabilities and Autistic Spectrum Disorder
(DoH, DES 2002)

This is guidance issued under section 7 of Local Authority Social Services Act 1970.

This guidance is for all staff who work with children with a learning disability.

It is thoughtfully written and comprehensive in its discussion of how services should address this important and sensitive matter.

The guidance makes clear the importance of organisational policies on the use of restrictive physical interventions. Such policies should also include reference to strategies for preventing the occurrence of behaviours which precipitate the use of physical intervention.

Organisations need to ensure that staff are sufficiently trained, that the use of physical interventions is minimised by the adoption of preventative strategies, that there is clear and complete recording and post incident management.

Where it is felt physical interventions may be required for a named individual they should be:-

O   Agreed in advance by a multidisciplinary or school team working in co-operation with the service user (where possible) and their parents

O   Detailed in writing

O   Include broader strategies to minimise the risk of behaviours occurring requiring physical interventions

O   Implemented under the supervision of a specially trained member of staff

O   Recorded so that the use of physical intervention can be reviewed

O   Risk assessments must be carried out

The use of physical interventions should always be designed to achieve outcomes that reflect the best interests of the child whose behaviour is of immediate concern.

Staff who are in care environments where physical interventions are part of the care plans of children they support are recommended to read this guidance.

Residential Care in Wales

The Care Standards Act 2000 gave the Welsh Assembly the responsibility to improve the quality of care services in Wales.

The Welsh Assembly established the Care Standards Inspectorate for Wales (CSIW) [Arolygiaeth Safonau Gofal Cymru (ASGC)] which has the responsibility to inspect all childrens (and adult) social care services.

Children's Homes (Wales) Regulations 2003

These were introduced by the Welsh Assembly.

The Regulations make direct reference to the home having:

- a statement of purpose (reg. 4)
- a policy on behaviour management (reg. 17)
- a policy of safeguarding children (reg. 16)
- a complaints procedure (reg. 24)

The Regulations are detailed and cover a range of management issues eg. levels of staffing, recording etc.

National Minimum Standards

National Minimum Standards have been generated by the Welsh Assembly Government. There are separate National Minimum Standards that relate to:

- Childrens homes (2002)
- Residential special schools (2003)
- Boarding schools (2003)

○ Students aged under 18 accommodated by further education colleges (2003)

All are very detailed and the CSIW/ASGC will use these, and the relevant regulations, as their measure when inspecting services.

In Summary

The importance of residential care for children is conveyed in a variety of ways, the increased expectation that all residential staff should be qualified is one example. The more detailed standards of care that have to be met also conveys how important residential child care is viewed.

12 FOSTERING AND ADOPTION

Fostering and adoption legislation is potentially confusing with Acts amending but not entirely replacing previous Acts.

The Adoption and Children Act 2002 is the product of the White Paper on adoption "Adoption – a new approach".

The Adoption and Children Act 2002 replaces most, but not quite all, of the Adoption Act 1976. The 2002 Act also amended the Children Act 1989 both in matters that relate to adoption and in matters not directly related but the 2002 Act was used as a vehicle to introduce the amendments.

This chapter will cover:

- Adoption Act 1976
- The Adoption and Children Act 2002
- Care Standards Act 2000
- The Fostering Services Regulations 2002 and Fostering Services (Wales) Regulations 2003
- Fostering Services, National Minimum Standards 2002
- National Minimum Standards for Fostering Services 2003
- The Children and Adoption Act 2006

Adoption Act 1976

Only Part IV of this Act still applies. Part IV deals with the legal status of adopted children. They are seen in law as being solely the children of the adoptive parents with equal rights to birth children. It is unlawful under this section to remove a child from the U.K. for the purpose of adoption elsewhere.

The Adoption and Children Act 2002

The Adoption and Children Act 2002 implements the following:

O   Puts the needs of children at the center of the adoption process by making the child's welfare the paramount consideration in all decisions to do with adoption (s.1).

O   Places a duty on local authorities to maintain an adoption service (s.3).

O   Places a new duty on local authorities to provide an adoption support service and a right for people affected by adoption to have an assessment of their needs to adoption support services (s.3 and s.4).

O   Establishes a review procedure for people who want to adopt and feel they have been turned down unfairly (s.8).

O   Provides for adoption orders to be made in favour of single people, unmarried couples and married couples (s.50 and s.51).

O   Cuts harmful delays in the adoption process by requiring courts to draw up timetables.

O   Improves legal controls on intercountry adoption, arranging adoption and the advertising of children for adoption (s.83-93 and other sections).

Care Standards Act 2000

This Act has far reaching effects on all statutory and voluntary care services and, in effect, simplifies and extends the ways in which they are inspected. The Act touches upon fostering and adoption services in the following ways:

O   Part III, Sections 43 to 53 detail new powers that the Commission for Social Care Inspection will have in relation to fostering and adoption services

O the Commission may advise the Secretary of State on any improvements it thinks are appropriate to fostering and adoption

O all fostering and adoption services, including local authority ones, must register with the Commission and the Commission may request a local authority to provide relevant information about its services and carry out inspections of the service and relevant premises, with the power to remove any documents or paperwork which it feels are relevant. It will then report back to the Secretary of State

O the Commission shall also report any failure of a service to the Secretary of State

O the Commission can recommend regulations for fostering and adoption, in particular, those which relate to:

- persons fit to work for local authorities in providing these services
- the fitness of premises used by the local authority.
- the management of fostering and adoption
- staffing levels for providing this service
- management and training issues

This all means that local authority services are brought under the inspection and regulation umbrella of one central body, reporting directly to the Secretary of State. Section 110 relates to privately fostered children who live at school during school holidays. Previously it was only children at non-statutory schools who had to have their welfare assessed but now this is extended to children at any school. They shall be assessed as though placed in a private foster placement.

Please note that all of the Commissions (CSCI) responsibility to register and inspect children's services will transfer to the new, enlarged Ofsted in 2007/2008.

The Fostering Services Regulations 2002

These are issued under the Children Act 1989 and the Care Standards Act 2000.

In their own right they are very detailed and address the following areas:-

- Fitness of the agency and the registered manager
- Conduct of the fostering service including arrangements for safeguarding children; promoting contact; support for foster carers; employment of suitable staff; record keeping etc.
- The selection of foster carers
- Management of placements including the supervision of placements and the provision of emergency placements

(This list is not exhaustive).

Fostering Services, National Minimum Standards 2002

These Standards support the Fostering Services Regulations. Even though the Regulations are detailed the Standards go into even more depth and clearly identify what is required (in quite concrete terms) of a fostering service.

The Standards closely follow the areas identified in the Regulations that have to be proved satisfactory.

Fostering Services in Wales

These are registered and inspected by the Care Standards Inspectorate for Wales (CSIW) [Arolygiaeth Safonau Gofal Cymru (ASGC)].

Fostering Services (Wales) Regulations 2003

These Regulations apply to the fostering agency and make clear the requirements they have to meet. The Regulations are very detailed and include:

- Fitness of the agency and the registered manager
- Conduct of the fostering service including arrangements for safeguarding children; promoting contact; support for foster carers; employment of suitable staff; record keeping etc.
- The selection of foster carers
- Management of placements including the supervision of placements and the provision of emergency placements

(This list is not exhaustive)

National Minimum Standards for Fostering Services 2003

These Standards support the Fostering Services (Wales) Regulations. Even though the Regulations are detailed the Standards go into even more depth and clearly identify what is required (in quite concrete terms) of a fostering service.

The Standards closely follow the areas identified in the Regulations that have to be proved satisfactory.

The Children and Adoption Act 2006

This Act received Royal Assent on 21st July 2006. It amends Children Act 1989, Adoption and Children Act 2002 and Adoption Act 1976

This Act provides courts with new powers to promote contact and enforce contact orders made under the Children Act 1989. This Act also addresses issues of inter-country adoption. In particular it creates a framework for restricting adoption from countries where there are concerns about adoption practices. Part 1 of the Act (about contact orders) applies to England and Wales while Part 2 (Inter-country Adoption) applies to England, Wales and Northern Ireland.

Part 1 addresses the needs of children and indeed families who are let down when parties fail to comply with contact arrangements. These new provisions are added to the Children Act 1989 as sections 11a to 11p.

Highlights include:

O Contact Activity Directions: not a decision about which parks to visit but directions for certain parties to attend activities to promote contact. This might include anger management or simply attending information meetings. Such directions cannot however order a person to attend mediation or receive medical or psychiatric treatment. Much of part 1 of the act sets out restrictions on imposing contact activity directions which is important because such directions are, in essence, a restriction on the freedom of someone who has not necessarily been convicted of a crime. The Secretary of State may authorise payments to facilitate a contact activity direction while the court may ask a CAFCASS officer to assess and monitor compliance with contact activity directions.

- Enforcement Orders: can be made when a person fails to comply with a contact activity direction. The act is specific about the use of these and also specifies penalties. A Warning Notice must be issued before enforcement can take place.

- Compensation of Financial Loss: If a person breaches a contact order this might result in another party incurring a financial loss. An example might be where a person travels a distance to see a child and the child's carer is deliberately out when they get there. The court may order the breacher to compensate the other party for that loss.

- Family Assistance Orders: Amending section 16 of the Children Act 89 these orders can now be used more often and for longer duration – up to 12 months. The "exceptional circumstances" requirement is also removed.

- Risk Assessments: A new section, 16a, is added to the Children Act 89. This requires CAFCASS officers to carry out risk assessments if, during private family law proceedings they suspect any risk of harm to the children involved.

Part 2: Adoption with a foreign element

The Secretary of State, in consultation with the National Assembly for Wales, may restrict the adoption of children from abroad. The Act specifies why such restrictions might be applied and also requires the Secretary of State to publish and maintain a "restricted list" of countries to which it applies. Justification for restriction must also be given and the list must be reviewed. Anyone bringing in a child from a restricted country is guilty of an offence.

Charges
Amending the Adoption and Children Act 2002, this Act allows the Secretary of State to set fees that prospective adopters should pay in order for inter-country adoptions to be properly processed.

Other Amendments
The 2002 Adoption and Children Act made it an offence to bring into the country a child that had been adopted less than 6 months before they were brought in. Section 14 of this Act amends section 83 of the 2002 Act to increase this period to twelve months.

When a local authority receives a notice of intention to adopt it has various tasks to perform: Section 14(3) of the new act clears up a potential point of confusion in this situation. The act repeals the "protected child" provisions of the Adoption Act 1976 but section 14(3) ensures that the child is not therefore automatically classed as being privately fostered.

This Act essentially modifies existing legislation to cater for changing adoption options in a modern world.

In Summary

The areas of adoption and fostering have gone through a rolling programme of review and reform.

The application of detailed and explicit standards should enable adoption agencies and fostering services to have a professional transparency that will enable them to allay any public concerns about their performance.

(13) YOUTH JUSTICE

Various legislation exists or has been specially enacted to facilitate the youth justice system.

- Police and Criminal Evidence Act 1984
- Criminal Justice and Public Order Act 1994 (This Act removed the right to silence resulting in the police caution being more complex to understand)
- Crime and Disorder Act 1998
- Youth Justice and Criminal Evidence Act 1999 (All the youth justice aspects of this Act were repealed and replaced the next year by the following Act)
- Powers of Criminal Courts (Sentencing) Act 2000
- Anti-social Behaviour Act 2003

Rather than detailing the Acts one by one and noting what additional aspects they introduced, this chapter will offer an overview.

The reader should be warned that this overview will not be exhaustive. There are now many options available to the criminal justice system in responding to youth crime.

Youth Justice Board

Youth Justice is currently overseen by the Youth Justice Board, an executive, non-departmental public body consisting of twelve people appointed by the Home Secretary. The Youth Justice Board was established under the Crime and Disorder Act 1998 and, in summary, is responsible for the following:

O   advising the Home Secretary on the operation of the youth justice system, particularly in relation to preventing youth crime

O   monitoring the performance of the youth justice system including Youth Courts, Youth Offending Teams (YOTs) and the provision of secure accommodation

O   advising the Home Secretary on drawing up standards for the work of YOTs and monitoring/publishing performance information

O   identifying and publicising good practice and commissioning research or funding it

The Board also has a role in promoting a new culture in society and youth crime intervention. Briefly, this revolves around preventive community based work and providing opportunities for young people.

The Board aims to reduce youth crime and speed up the judicial process by various methods and has powers to intervene at a local level where local teams are thought to be failing.

In its first year the Board established, via local authorities, multi disciplinary Youth Offending Teams. These include staff from social services, probation, police, education welfare and health.

Police Powers

In recent years the police have been given various powers which could be used in respect of young people.

Removal of Suspected Truant
(Crime and Disorder Act 1998, s.16)

If a police officer believes a person in a public place is:

O   of compulsory school age

O   and absent from school without permission

The police officer can take the child from the public place to either the child's school or a place designated by the local authority as a building to which such children should initially be brought.

Dispersal of Groups
(Anti-social Behaviour Act 2003, s. 30)

If there is a local area where anti-social behaviour caused by groups of people is seen as a problem a senior police officer can issue an authorisation notice. This authorisation notice includes:

O   the relevant area

O   specifies a time limit (up to a maximum of six months)

O   identifies the nature of the problem

As a result of the authorisation notice, uniformed police officers within that location can order groups of people to disperse. A person who contravenes a direction from a police officer operating under the powers of an authorisation notice commits an arrestable offence.

Removal of Person Aged Under 16 to Place of Residence
(Anti-social Behaviour Act 2003)

A uniformed police officer has the power to convey a young person to their place of residence if the following conditions apply:

O   The police officer reasonably believes the person is aged under 16.

O   The young person is not under the effective control of a responsible adult.

O   The young person is presently in a location to which an authorisation notice applies.

O   It is between 9pm and 6am.

Pre Court Options

If a young person is viewed as being at risk of offending then the police, local authority or registered social landlord may be able to intervene without the person getting fully enmeshed in the youth justice system.

Acceptable Behaviour Contract (ABC)

An Acceptable Behaviour Contract (ABC) is a voluntary agreement between a person involved in anti-social behaviour and a local agency (such as police or housing) whose role is to reduce such behaviour.

The contract details the behaviours the person has been involved in and which they agree not to repeat.

The contract should state consequences if the person breaks the contract eg. an ASBO or moves towards a possession order if the person lives in social housing.

Anti-Social Behaviour Order (ASBO)

Originally introduced by the Crime and Disorder Act 1998 (s.1). This has been enhanced by amendments introduced by the Anti-social Behaviour Act 2003

This is a civil order, made through a magistrates court, but higher courts can also issue ASBOs.

ASBOs can be issued to persons over the age of 10 years who have acted in an anti-social manner and the order is necessary to protect others from anti-social activity. An ASBO prohibits that person from doing anything described in the order.

Breach of an order is an arrestable, criminal offence.

Reprimand

A reprimand is a formal verbal warning given by a police officer to a young person who admits they are guilty to a minor first offence.

Final Warning

A Final Warning is a formal verbal warning given by a police officer to a young person who admits guilt to a first or second offence. The young person is also assessed to determine the causes of their offending behaviour and a programme of activities is identified to address them.

Local Child Curfew Order
(Crime and Disorder Act 1998 s.14, as amended by Criminal Justice and Police Act 2001 s. 48 and 49).

A local authority or local police authority can ban children aged under 16 from being in a public place between 9pm and 6am unless they are with a responsible adult. The ban is a blanket ban. The local authority or police force apply to the Home Secretary for a Local Child Curfew Order to be agreed. If a child violates the Order and is picked up by the police this could result in the child being made subject to a Child Safety Order.

Child Safety Order
(Crime and Disorder Act 1998, s.11)

Where a child, aged under 10 engages in actions that would be considered an offence for a person aged over 10 then the local authority may apply to a magistrates court for a Child Safety Order. This can last for 90 days and the child will be supervised by a social worker or Youth Offending Team worker. Other conditions can be specified. If the Child Safety Order is violated by the child it could result in application for a Care Order (under the Children Act 1989).

Sentences to the Community

Community Rehabilitation and Punishment Order [Combination Order]
(Powers of Criminal Courts (sentencing) Act 2000, s.51)

Courts can apply this order to people aged 16 or over. It is the equivalent of a Supervision Order. It can include an Intensive Supervision and Surveillance Programme (ISSP), and a requirement to perform unpaid work for between 40 to 100 hours.

Community Rehabilitation Order/Probation Order
(Powers of Criminal Courts (Sentencing) Act 2000, s.41)

Courts can only apply this to people aged 16 or more. The young person will be supervised by the Youth Offending team and could well engage in activities aimed at repairing the harm caused by their offence. It could include an Intensive Supervision and Surveillance Programme (ISSP).

Community Punishment Order
(Powers of Criminal Courts (Sentencing) Act 2000, s.46 to s.50)

Courts can only apply this to people aged 16 or more. The young person has to complete unpaid community work for a period set between 40 to 240 hours.

Supervision will be through the Probation Service Community Service Team.

Supervision Order
(Powers of Criminal Courts (Sentencing) Act 2000 s.34; s.63 to s.67; schedules 6 and 7)

The Supervision Order can include a range of conditions including participation in an Intensive Supervision and Surveillance Programme (ISSP), curfew or residence requirements.

The young person will be under the supervision of the Youth Offending Team (YOT) and may well include programmes to address their offending behaviour. A Supervision order can last three years.

Action Plan Order
(Crime and Disorder Act s.69, s.70 and Schedule 5)

This is an intensive community based programme, lasting three months. They can be issued to young people aged 10 to 17. Conditions can be applied, including restitution for harm done or attending education or training activities.

Attendance Centre Order
(Powers of Criminal Courts (Sentencing) Act 2000 s.60 to s.62)

This option is available to courts where the offender is aged 10-20. The Attendance Centre is usually managed by the police. The young person will normally be required to attend the centre each Saturday for a few hours. The maximum number of hours that can be required in the order is 36, with lower limits for younger people.

Reparation Orders
(Powers of Criminal Courts (Sentencing) Act 2000, s.73 to s.75 and Schedule 8)

A court can issue this Order to a person aged 10 to 17. The young person could be ordered to make reparation to a specified person (eg the victim of the crime) or the community at large. The time commitment for the young person has a maximum of 24 hours. Supervision is usually through Youth Offending Team.

Curfew Orders
(Powers of Criminal Courts (Sentencing) Act 2000, s.37 to s.40)

Courts can issue these to people aged 10 or more. The Order can last for three months for young people aged 10 to 15 (inclusive) or six months for a person aged 16 or more. The person can be required to observe a curfew each day lasting from two to twelve hours for the length of the Order.

Drug Treatment and Testing Order
(Powers of Criminal Courts (Sentencing) Act 2000, s52 to s.58)

This order can be issued to people aged 16 or more. The person is required to attend a drug treatment service and this will include regular testing. The person needs to be willing to comply. If they don't the court will be notified and will then reconsider their options.

Referral Order
(Powers of Criminal Courts (Sentencing) Act 2000 s.16 to s.32)

If a young person aged under 18 appears before a magistrates court and certain conditions are met, the court can make a referral Order. The conditions to be met include:

o   the person pleads guilty

o   the person has no previous convictions

o   the court feels custody is not appropriate but a punishment is required

The Referral Order means the young person is referred to a Youth Offending Panel.

The Youth Offending Panel consists of a professional from a YOT and two lay members (members of the public who have volunteered their time to be on this Panel). The Panel works with the young person and their parents/carers to decide on a punishment. This commonly includes some aspect of restorative justice and activities aimed at addressing the offending behaviour. This contract lasts from three to twelve months.

The Youth Offending Panel is intended to balance various competing demands, these include:

- the need to recognise an offence has occurred and an individual should accept responsibility
- recognise that the offender is a child and they have their own needs
- the criminal justice system should be arranged such that the young person senses their involvement
- beyond punishment is the aim of reducing the risk of re-offending

Parenting Contracts and Orders (in respect of offending behaviour or anti-social behaviour)
(Crime and Disorder Act 1988, s.8; Anti-Social Behaviour Act 2003, s.25 to s.29)

Parenting Contracts have been introduced by the Anti-social Behaviour Act 2003, s.25. They are intended to formalise agreements between the parents of a young person who offends and YOT's. The parent or carer will be expected to attend a parenting programme aimed at enhancing their parenting skills. The Parenting Contract, whilst having a statutory basis, is voluntary. However, if a parent refused to co-operate with a parenting contract the YOT can go to court and request a Parenting Order is issued.

A Parenting Order should only be issued if attempts at making a Parenting Contract have failed. The core requirement of a Parenting Order is that the parent attends a parenting programme. Additional requirements can be added, where they are relevant to reducing the risk of their child re-offending. For example, the parent may be required to ensure that the child is at home during certain hours at night and is effectively supervised.

Potentially, a Parenting Order can have conditions that require the parent to participate in a residential programme, but this will only be agreed where there are pressing reasons to require this.

To breach a Parenting Order is an offence.

Intensive Supervision and Surveillance Programme (ISSP)

This is not an order. A persistent young offender who receives a Supervision order or Community Rehabilitation Order may be required to follow an ISSP. There are other routes onto an ISSP as well.

An ISSP consists of:

- Supervision. A minimum of 25 hours programmed contact time, which could include education, addressing offending behaviour; reparation to the victim or community amongst other things
- Surveillance. This can take a number of forms including electronic tagging; escorting to scheduled activities, telephone calls to check a person is where they should be using 'voice print' to confirm identity.

Custodial Sentences

Custodial sentences should only be used where the seriousness of the offence merits custody or the young person is a persistent offender.

 In Summary

Youth crime is a major political issue. All governments introduce initiatives to address public concerns. This results in changes to the legislative and practice framework of youth justice on a continuing basis.

(14) LEAVING CARE

Research spanning the last 25 years has shown that young people from the care system are significantly more likely to become homeless, unemployed, under achieve academically and are at increased risk of entering the criminal justice system. Current average ages in the UK for leaving home are between 20 and 22, whereas young people leaving care are aged between 16 and 18.

Care leavers need guidance and support before, during and after the point at which they leave care. The Children Act 1989 in its original section 24 stated what was required from local authorities but the outcomes for care leavers did not really improve during the 1990s. In the light of this, the Children (Leaving Care) Act 2000, was introduced. It was implemented in 2001.

This chapter will cover:

- Children (Leaving Care) Act 2000
- Housing Act 1996
- Homeless Act 2002

Children (Leaving Care) Act 2000

Many of the provisions of this Act are inserted into the Children Act 1989. Many of these are additional sections. However, section 24 of the Children Act 1989 is completely replaced by a new section 24. This new section 24 is supported by additional sections 24A to 24D.

The provisions include:

O 16 and 17 year old care leavers will not be able to claim Income Support, Job Seekers Allowance or Housing Benefit. This applies whether they leave care or not. This means that the local authority will have a duty to assess and meet their needs, both financially and in terms of welfare, education, development etc

O each child will have a Pathway Plan, a sort of leaving care plan which they will have a role in putting together.

O there is a duty to appoint a personal advisor to each young person leaving care. The personal advisors role includes, providing advice and support and co-ordinating the Pathway Plan

O there is a duty for the local authority to maintain contact until 21 or re-establish contact if it is lost

O there is a duty to assist with vacation accommodation for care leavers in higher education

O the responsible local authority is the one in which they were in care when they left

O duty to provide support to 18 to 21 year olds, including assistance with costs involved with accessing education or training or work. This to last beyond 21 if a course continues

'Eligible' and 'Relevant' children.

To be 'Eligible' for these services a young person must have been in the care system for at least 13 weeks, although this can be a series of shorter care episodes added up since the age of 14. Children who live at home and have agreed respite stays will almost certainly be excluded. 'Eligible' children remain in care until 18.

'Relevant' children are subject to the same rules and entitlements but have chosen to leave care at 16 or 17. As they still cannot claim basic benefits the local authority will have a duty to maintain them.

The Children (Leaving Care) (England) Regulations 2001 and the Children (Leaving Care) (Wales) Regulations 2001 came into effect in 2001. They are supported by guidance. This guidance is detailed and applied. Staff working in this area need to have sight of the guidance that is relevant to them.

Using Relevant Legislation

For the worker assisting a young person with the transition from the care system, a knowledge of housing legislation is useful. Local authorities are expected to have joint strategies with local housing departments to enable young people to move smoothly from the care system to housing of good quality, preferably with support available. More housing associations and foyers are providing supported housing for young people leaving care, and in many cases local housing authorities have nomination rights to such projects or else many can be accessed directly.

The Housing Act 1996, as amended by the Homelessness Act 2002, has confirmed the importance of housing authorities working to arrange accommodation for people who:

O   are homeless or under threat of homelessness
O   are vulnerable

Housing Act 1996

This Act directs housing authorities in the way they should assist vulnerable, homeless people who present to them. It also enacted many new measures including:

O   the introduction of Registered Social Landlords; who could receive government funding for housing schemes without having to be full housing associations
O   setting standards for Houses in Multiple Occupation (HMO's)
O   tenants' rights
O   the controversial reform of assured tenancies and other types of tenancy in council housing
O   land reform
O   housing allocation

- anti-social behaviour
- homelessness legislation

Homelessness Act 2002

This Act amends, but does not replace, the Housing Act 1996. The intention of the amendments to the Housing Act 1996 are clearly to remove rigidities within the 1996 Act.

The changes introduced by the Homelessness Act 2002 aim to tackle homelessness by enabling housing authorities to facilitate access to stable accommodation for people who are eligible, homeless through no fault of their own and have a priority need.

 In Summary

It has been increasingly recognised that young people who leave care need assistance and support of various forms. Whilst local authorities have had powers for some time such that they could support care leavers the introduction of the Children (Leaving Care) Act has enhanced the rights of care leavers and, so it is hoped, will strengthen the life opportunities of all people leaving care.

15   EARLY YEARS: CHILD MINDING AND CHILDCARE

There have been two major changes in law and policy in relation to early years provision that are relevant to this chapter:

o There has been increased emphasis on the educational development of young children

o The legislative basis for childcare in respect of England and Wales is now distinct and separate

Additionally, there has also been the broad policy move towards safeguarding all children and this applies equally to young children.

This chapter will cover:

o Childcare Act 2006

o Children Act 1989 (as amended by the Care Standards Act 2000 and the Childcare Act 2006)

o School Standards and Framework Act 1998

Childcare in England

Childcare in England has been consolidated into the Childcare Act 2006. The sections of the Children Act 1989 that relate specifically to early years provision in respect of England, have been deleted. A similar process has been followed in respect of the School Standards and Framework Act 1998; the sections that relate to childcare in these two Acts have been amended so they only relate to Wales.

Childcare Act 2006

The Childcare Act 2006 introduces new statutory responsibilities onto local authorities in respect of the care of pre school children.

Part 1 of the 2006 Act relates to English local authorities, Part 2 relates to Wales.

English Local Authorities

All English local authorities must (s.1):

- improve the well being of young children in their area
- reduce inequalities between young children in their area

Well being is described in terms of:

- physical and mental health and emotional well being
- protection from harm and neglect
- education, training and recreation
- their contribution to society
- social and economic well being

The local authority must make arrangements to (s.3):

- provide early childhood services in an integrated manner
- identify parents who may not take advantage of early childhood services and encourage them to engage

Local authorities, NHS organisations and Jobcentre Plus have a duty to work together to provide services to parents (s.4).
The local authority has a duty to:

- assess how much childcare is available in their area and decide if this is sufficient for the needs of the local people. This must be repeated every three years (s.11)

- provide or arrange for childcare services for parents who are in work or parents who are in education or training leading to work (s.6)

- provide or arrange early years provision that is free in line with any guidance issued by the Secretary of State (s.7)

- provide a service giving information and advice to parents about the provision of childcare in their area (s.12)

- provide information and training to childcare providers

The regulations and specifics for local authorities carrying out the above duties came into force on 1st April 2007. They are to be found in a statutory instrument entitled "The Childcare Act 2006 (Childcare Assessments) (England) Regulations 2007. Ref 2007 No. 463. They can be found with a simple internet search on the title.

Regulations governing how local authorities will provide information, advice and training to childcare providers in England can be found in the Statutory Instrument entitled "The Childcare Providers (Information, Advice and Training) Regulations 2007. Ref 2007 No. 1797.

This duty and therefore these regulations, will apply to all registrations by September 2008. Prior to this, only certain categories of registration are covered. As always, further study of the actual regulations are advised if this is your area of interest.

A child is a young child until the 1st September that follows the child's fifth birthday.

Early years provision relates to care of a young child. Childcare relates to supervised care of a child but does not include school hours education and does not include health care nor care in the childs own home by a family member etc. (s.18-20).

The Chief Inspector of Schools has the duty of registering, inspecting and reporting on childcare provision in England. (Confusingly the organisation the Chief Inspector leads is called Ofsted.)

In line with requirements issued by the Secretary of State, all people who provide early years childminding must register on the early years register carried by Ofsted (s.33).

Early years providers (eg. nurseries) must also register but the registration is in respect of the premises (s.34). As always there are exemptions to register, one of which is schools that provide early years provision for children aged 3 to 5.

The Secretary of State is given the duty of generating a learning curriculum titled the Early Years Foundation Stage (EYFS). The EYFS will also contain welfare requirements which relate to safeguarding children, the qualifications of staff involved in childcare etc (s.39, 41 and 43).

The Early Years Foundation Stage must be applied by early years providers (s.40).

Individuals who provide child minding for children aged 5 to 8 and people who own an organisation that provides childcare for children aged 5 to 8 must also register with Ofsted (s.52 and 53). Again, there are exemptions to register (schools that meet certain conditions).

The Secretary of State is given the power to make regulations governing how later years providers carry out their activities (s.59). If these regulations are generated, all later years providers (child minders, childcare clubs and schools that provide out of hours childcare) must observe them (whether they have needed to register or not).

Later years provisions is defined as care for a child who is aged 5 or more on the 1st September.

The Chief Inspector has the responsibility to inspect and provide reports on early years and later year provision in England (s.49, 50, 60, 61 etc).

The Chief Inspector is also given a range of powers if there are concerns that a childcare provider is not working to the standards expected of them.

Childcare in Wales

The legislative basis for childcare in Wales is drawn from a number of Acts. The principle Acts are as follows:

Childcare Act 2006

Part 2 of the 2006 Act applies specifically to Wales.

Welsh Local Authorities

Every local authority must ensure (as far as practicable) that there is sufficient childcare for:

- parents in work or returning to work
- parents undertaking education or training leading to work

The local authority must take into account:

- childcare that is suitable for disabled children
- childcare involving the use of the Welsh language (s.22)

Local authorities must:

- establish and maintain a service providing information, advice or assistance to parents about the provision of childcare in their area (s.27).

The Welsh Assembly is given the power to introduce regulations requiring local authorities to assess the sufficiency of the provision of childcare in their area (s.26).

Children Act 1989 (as amended by the Care Standards Act 2000 and the Childcare Act 2006)

The Care Standards Act 2000 contains, in section 79, an addition to Part X of the Children Act 1989. This is called Part XA and relates to child minding and day care for children in Wales. Initially this part is a clarification of Part X, especially in terms of definitions of child minders and the work of Nannies although the word 'Nanny' does not appear. Further clarification is given about who can be approved as a child minder and what constitutes child minding. These are fairly long definitions and the actual text should be consulted.

The registration and inspection of child minders and day care for young children is made the responsibility of the Welsh National Assembly. The Welsh Assembly delegated this task to the Care Standards Inspectorate for Wales (CSIW).

The Act allows the Assembly to make regulations about child minders in such areas as:

O   the welfare and development of children cared for
O   qualifications and training
O   the keeping of records

The Act further enforces the requirement to register and deals with this in detail including refusals to register, suspension, resignation from the register and measures to be taken by local authorities to protect children in emergencies.

School Standards and Framework Act 1998

This is a very wide ranging Act which covers many aspects of education from early years to further education. It does however, have the following to say about nursery education in Wales:

O   section 117 defines nursery education as being full or part time education for children who have not yet reached compulsory school age
O   section 118 states the duty of the LEA to make nursery education available
O   the LEA shall establish Early Years Development and Childcare Partnerships to review the sufficiency of nursery education in the area.

 In Summary

In England there has been a major change in the legislative duties placed on local authorities in terms of early years education and childcare. The Childcare Act

2006 consolidates childcare legislation in respect of England.

In Wales, the Assembly has the power to issue regulations relating to various aspects of childcare legislation.

(16) EDUCATION

Since the subject of education has a high political profile new policy developments and pieces of legislation are regularly introduced. This chapter covers the major Acts relevant to work in the field of education.

Rather than going through each Act in order, this chapter summarises the legislation in terms of themes and issues within education.

Towards the end of this chapter, the newest Act relating to education is covered – The Education and Inspections Act 2006. Reference is also made to a Bill which is currently going through Parliament – the Education and Skills Bill 2007/2008.

The National Curriculum

The basic features of the National Curriculum were first laid down in the Education Reform Act 1988. Further details are outlined in Part V of the Education Act 1996. The Education Act 2002 has consolidated the aims of the National Curriculum.

The National Curriculum is made up of: English, mathematics, science, technology, history, geography, music, art and design, PE, citizenship (for secondary school pupils) and a modern foreign language (for secondary pupils). The curriculum is organised in four key stages which are as follows:

	Pupil's Ages	**Year Groups**
Early Years Foundation Stage	3 to 5	Early Years/ Reception
Key Stage 1	5 to 7	1-2
Key Stage 2	7 to 11	3-6
Key Stage 3	11 to 14	7-9
Key Stage 4	14 to 16	10-11

The Early Years Foundation Stage does not have formal areas of study. Instead it seeks to cultivate an inclusive, positive and responsive learning environment.

From Key Stage 1 onwards, there are programmes of study which set out what pupils should be taught.

Pupils should be assessed at four key points, for most children these assessments will be at age 7, 11, 14 and 16.

Each school must report assessment results to their parents and publish the results in its prospectus and governor's annual report to parents.

Careers Education and Guidance

This is covered by Part VII of the Education Act 1997 which requires schools to:-

O   provide programmes of careers education to all pupils in Years 9 to 11

O   work with careers services to ensure that pupils have access to comprehensive and up-to-date careers information

O   provide access to careers services to enable them to provide services to pupils

Children with Special Educational Needs

The Education Act 1996 sets out the framework for children with special educational needs to attend mainstream schools. Under the Act school governing bodies have the following duties:-

O   make every effort to see that the necessary special arrangements are made for any pupil who has special educational needs

O   make sure that the 'responsible person' makes all staff who are likely to teach the pupil aware of those needs. The 'responsible person' is generally the head, but may be the chair of the governing body or a governor appointed to take that responsibility

O   make sure that the teachers are aware of the importance of identifying pupils who have special educational needs and of providing appropriate teaching

O   consult the LEA and the governing bodies of other schools when it seems necessary to co-ordinate special educational teaching in the area

O   make arrangements to allow pupils with special needs to join in the everyday activities of the school as far as is practical

O   report each year to parents on their policy for pupils with special educational needs

Under the Education (Special Educational Needs) (Information) Regulations 1999, governing bodies must publish information about their special needs policies. These policies must be made freely available to parents.

The requirements of the Education Act 1996 to integrate disabled children into mainstream schools have been strengthened by the Special Educational Needs and Disability Act 2001. The 2001 Act inserts new sections into the Education Act 1996. One of these sections makes it a duty to educate disabled pupils in mainstream schools.

Discipline Issues

Control of Pupils

Section 550A of the Education Act 1996 clarifies the powers of teachers and other staff who have lawful control or charge of pupils to use reasonable force to prevent pupils causing injury of damage, committing a crime or causing disruption.

The Schools Standards and Framework Act 1998 includes provision for:

O   outlawing corporal punishment for all pupils'

O   requiring head teachers to determine measures to prevent all forms of bullying

Governing bodies have duties to agree a statement of general principles from which the school's discipline policy is drawn up by the head teacher. The governing body may include principles of bullying prevention in the statement.

Under the School Standards and Framework Act 1998, the head teacher is responsible for taking measures to secure good behaviour in line with the written statement of general principles prepared by the governing body.

The Education Act 2002 and associated Regulations governs the exclusion of pupils from maintained schools. "Exclude" means exclude on disciplinary grounds. There are two categories of exclusion: fixed period (suspension) or permanent (expulsion). Pupils may also be excluded from the school premises for the duration of lunchtime break between the morning and afternoon school sessions.

Only the head teacher (or acting head teacher) has the power to exclude a pupil from school. He or she may not delegate that power to someone else. The head teacher may exclude a pupil for one or more fixed periods not exceeding a total of 45 school days in any one school year. He or she may also exclude a pupil permanently.

In all cases the head teacher must promptly:

- inform the pupil's parent of the period of the exclusion, or that the exclusion is permanent
- give the reasons for the exclusion
- advise the parent that he or she may make representations about the exclusion to the governing body's discipline committee
- advise the parent how his or her representations may be made

Where a child has been excluded, the LEA or governing body of the school could consider whether to offer a parenting contract to the parent. The parenting contract is voluntary. It could include a range of requirements such as the parent attending a parenting programme. The intention of the contract is to improve the pupils behaviour at school partly through addressing any underlying causes.

When a child is permanently excluded from school or receives more than one fixed term exclusion in twelve months, the LEA should consider whether to apply to a court for a parenting order. Parenting orders compel a parent to co-operate where they have been unwilling to engage on a voluntary basis to address their child's behaviour. Parenting orders can have various requirements attached, such as the parent must attend a parenting programme. If a parent does not comply with an Order, the LEA could return to court where a fine of up to £1,000 could be levied on the parent.

The Education Act 2002 has been amended by the Education Act 2005, such that the governing body of a school has the power to direct excluded pupils to alternative education provision.

School Attendance

Under section 7 of the Education Act 1996, the parent is responsible for making sure that their child of compulsory school age receives suitable full time education. This can be by regular attendance at school or by education the parents arrange.

When a parent knows that their child is not attending school, then the parent is committing an offence under section 444 of the Education Act 1996.

Under the Education (Pupil Registration) Regulations 1995, the governing body are responsible for making sure that two registers are kept: one for admissions and one for attendance. An admission register is the school's roll. It must give details of every pupil currently on roll at the school including their full name, date of birth and the name and address of at least one parent or guardian in case of emergency. The attendance register has to be called at the start of each morning and afternoon session and must show whether each pupil registered at the school is present or absent. The attendance register must indicate whether the absence of a pupil of compulsory school age was authorised or unauthorised. Only the school can authorise absence: parents do not have this power.

LEAs are responsible for initiating actions where it becomes clear a child is not attending school regularly. At agreed intervals, the governing body must give the LEA the name and address of every pupil who does not go to school regularly, or who has been continuously away for at least two weeks (if the absence is unauthorised). The governing body should, however, inform the LEA if a pupil is likely to be absent for more than four weeks on medical grounds. The cause of absence must be shown if known. The LEA must also be told if a pupil of compulsory school age has been taken off a roll because they will be taught at home by their parents. This is to make sure that the LEA has the chance to assess whether this will be a suitable alternative to school.

Where a child's attendance at school is poor the LEA will need to consider how to intervene. Options include:

- Offer a parenting contract to the parent. This is a voluntary agreement and could include a commitment from the parent to attend a parenting programme. If a parenting contract did not work and the child was still absent from school, then the LEA could move to stronger interventions.
- Parents could be served with a parenting notice (basically a fine but paid to the LEA).
- If parents did not pay the parenting notice they could be prosecuted under section 444 of the Education Act 1996. If the child continued to be absent from school the parents could also be prosecuted under section 444 of the 1996 Act.

As a result of amendments introduced by the Education Act 2005, parents are also responsible for ensuring their child attends alternative education provision in the same way that parents are responsible for their child to attend school.

Length of the School Day and Term

The dates of school terms and holidays are decided by the LEA for community and voluntary controlled schools and by the governing body for foundation and voluntary aided schools.

The governing body decide when sessions should begin and end on each school day. Sessions must allow enough lesson time to deliver a broad and balanced curriculum that includes the National Curriculum and religious education. Current guidance on the levels of lesson time are contained in Circular 7/90 "Management of the School Day". This recommends:

o   21 hours for pupils aged 5 to 7

o   23 and half hours for pupils aged 8 to 11

o   24 hours for pupils aged 12 to 16

School Meals

The School Standards and Framework Act 1998 gives the Secretary of State the power to make regulations setting out compulsory minimum nutritional standards for school lunches. The Act places a duty on LEAs and schools to provide school lunches for pupils to buy on request.

School Inspections

The Education Act 2005 reforms the school inspection system.

The 2005 Act repeals all of the School Inspections Act 1996 but then re-enacts various sections and introduces amended or entirely new sections.

Her Majesty's Chief Inspectorate of Schools in England is established through the 2005 Act. (This organisation is also known as Ofsted.)

The Chief Inspector has the responsibility and the power to inspect schools and to then produce reports. Inspections are expected to have a 'lighter touch' and often to give less notice. Schools that give cause for concern can be categorised as either:

- ○ requiring special measures since they are failing to provide an acceptable standard of education and the capacity to improve is not demonstrated
- ○ requiring significant improvements

This Act also establishes the office of Her Majesty's Chief Inspector for Education and Training in Wales. The Chief Inspector is given the responsibility to inspect schools in Wales and to produce reports following inspections of schools. The Chief Inspector has to report annually to the Welsh Assembly.

Promoting the Educational Achievement of Looked After Children

In the late 1990s the Department of Health initiative Quality Protects highlighted how looked after children had very poor academic results compared to their peers. In spite of the Quality Protects initiative there has been little progress in this important area of work.

The Every Child Matters, Change for Children initiative has moved everything into a higher gear. Local authorities, children's services and schools need to do all they can to support looked after children improve their educational achievements.

Under s.22(3)(a) of the Children Act 1989 (as amended by s.52 of the Children Act 2004), the local authority has a duty to promote the educational achievement of looked after children.

This is, in part, directed by the Education (Admission of Looked After Children) (England) Regulations 2006 which require admission authorities in England to give priority to looked after children. These regulations also set out limited exceptions to this requirement. The regulations are a Statutory Instrument, Ref 2006 No. 128. They can be found with a simple internet search on the title.

Statutory Guidance On the Duty On Local Authorities to Promote the Educational Achievement of Looked After Children Under Section 52 of the Children Act 2004

This statutory guidance was issued in 2005 under s.7 of the Local Authority Social Services Act 1970 it applies to England only. It makes clear the need for local authorities to energetically work to improve Looked After Children's educational achievement. This includes:

○ Active strategic leadership that focuses on education for looked after children from the Director of Children's Services and the lead council member

○ Joint Area Reviews (JARs) will highlight how effectively agencies are working together to secure positive outcomes for disadvantaged children

○ The importance of high quality Personal Education Plans that reflects the looked after child's aspirations and learning needs

○ Foster carers or other children services workers attend parents evening and other meetings

○ Foster carers or other children's services workers mediate on behalf of a looked after child when they have problems at school

○ The looked after child is actively supported to participate in high quality learning experiences

○ Work in partnership with designated teachers and other education professionals

○ Wherever possible, work in partnership with parents

○ Schools need to recognise the importance of the role of designated teachers

○ Children's services to support foster carers and residential support workers recognise that supporting children attend school and succeed in education is one of their key roles

○ Children services to do all they can to avoid disrupting a child's education by maintaining educational continuity as far as possible

Education (Admission of Looked After Children) (England) Regulations 2006

Where a school is over subscribed (more applications than places available) the admissions authority must give priority to relevant looked after children in deciding who to enroll.

Safeguarding and Promoting the Welfare of Pupils

The governing bodies of maintained schools, the governing bodies of Further Education institutions and LEA's have a duty to safeguard and promote the welfare of children when exercising their functions (s.175, Education Act 2002). Section 157 of the Education Act 2002 places the same duties on the proprietors of independent schools.

Safeguarding includes aspects such as pupil health and safety, addressing bullying, drug and substance misuse etc. Safeguarding also relates to having child protection policies and procedures in place. It is not the responsibility of schools to investigate child abuse allegations, that is for the police and social services to do.

For pupils who are in boarding schools the Care Standards Act 2000 (as amended by the Health and Social Care (Community Health and Standards) Act 2003), establishes the system for the regulation and inspection of schools that provide accommodation for children. The Commission for Social Care Inspection undertakes inspections and apply the relevant National Minimum Standards (NMS) (eg. NMS – Boarding schools; NMS – Residential Special Schools; NMS – Accommodation of Students under Eighteen by Further Education Colleges). At present, CSCI inspections relate to the child care aspects of boarding schools. As a result of the Children Act 2004 future inspections will be joint (Ofsted and CSCI) until the new enlarged Ofsted takes responsibility for inspecting all children's services in 2007/2008.

Guidance on the Education of Children Looked After By Local Authorities (National Assembly for Wales 2001)

This guidance is part of the broader policy initiative in Wales titled "Children First". The 2001 guidance highlights the need to support looked after children to benefit from the education system and anticipates that an increasing proportion of looked after children will leave school with more GCSEs.

The roles of key professionals are discussed including the importance of foster carers and residential staff supporting the child attend school, attending parents evenings and facilitating contact with the child's parents (where relevant).

Education and Inspections Act 2006

This Act received Royal Assent on 8th November 2006. It amends the Education Act 1996, School Standards and Frameworks Act 1998, Education Act 2002 and Education Act 2005.

Overview

This Act is huge and complex and covers some areas which do not, directly, affect the welfare of children and young people. It is not appropriate, in this slim volume to pull it apart in detail so we shall simply give a very brief summary of its ten Parts. It covers England and Wales to slightly varying degrees except for section 162 and some general principles which are UK wide.

The Act mainly implements proposals from the white paper "Higher Standards, Better Schools for All (Cm 6677)".

As mentioned, the Act is made up of Ten Parts, concerned with the following areas:

Part 1
New duties on Local Education Authorities (LEAs) to promote children fulfilling their potential, diversity, and choice. Parents views about school provision to be considered and children not receiving education to be identified. Other new duties are drawn from the Green Paper Youth Matters (CM 6629).

Part 2
Abolishes School Organisational Committees, passing their responsibilities to LEAs. Imposes various minimum establishment requirements and sets out a new statutory procedure for schools to acquire a foundation.

Part 3
Various further organisational requirements within schools including establishment of Parent Councils and a duty to have regard to the Children and Young People's Plan. Also bans interviewing for admission to maintained schools.

Part 4
New powers for LEAs to tackle failing schools. They may now force such schools to federate or take a partner to affect school

improvement. Also addresses formal warning legislation for failing schools.

Part 5
Implements the proposals of white paper *14 – 19 Education and Skills* (CM 6476), to assist 14 to 19 year old learners in accessing qualifications.

Part 6
A duty on LEAs to promote sustainable forms of transport and free travel to certain pupils. Part 6 also permits nutritional standards to be applied to food and drink provided on school and LEA premises.

Part 7
Provides new powers for teachers to discipline pupils, extends parenting orders and contracts, and makes parents responsible for children in the first five days of exclusion.

Part 8
Major organisational reform of inspection services, vastly simplifying it. Creates a new Office of Standards in Education, Childrens Services and Skills and the post of Her Majesty's Chief Inspector Education, Childrens Services and Skills. This office covers the previously held duties of a number of services and inspectorates and brings them together "under one roof".

Part 9
This deals with miscellaneous aspects required to make the Act function in law.

Part 10
Deals with the role of the National Assembly of Wales in the Act with particular reference to Section 179 which is chiefly about the daily functioning of schools.

Education and Skills Bill 2007- 2008
Covers: England

This bill is very much part of the Government's Children and Young Person's Plan arising from the broad-reaching Every Child Matters agenda and, more specifically the findings of the Leitch Review on adult skills.

The aim of the Bill is to "encourage" more young people to participate in learning, post 16 although in actual fact encouragement does not really come into it as we see in the summary below:

<u>Main Areas of the Bills Intentions</u>

- Raise the age that young people remain in education and training. A duty on young people to participate and on their parents to assist them.

- Employers to have a duty to give young people day-release to attend training if they do not provide it themselves.

- Local Authorities also to have a duty to ensure young people participate in education and training and also to provide the support service currently known as Connexions.

- Local Authorities must assess the education and training needs of 16 to 19 year olds who have special educational needs.

- The Learning and Skills Council have a duty to secure courses for people over the age of 19.

At the time of writing, this is a Bill and is not law yet. However, once created as an Act the basic intentions will, in all probability be the same. There has been some opposition to what basically amounts to a raising of the school leaving age. The argument is that young people who are not engaged with the school system will hardly thrive if made to remain in it. The additional training requirement may go some way to alleviating this however as disenfranchised young people can, in theory at least get into work based training and earn some money. Time will, as always, tell.

Special Educational Needs Bill 2008
Territorial Extent: England and Wales

This Bill proposes to amend the Education Act 1996 relating to the way information about outcomes and services to children with special educational needs are published. The Bill proposes to highlight good practice within schools and local education authorities by ensuring that such practice is brought to wider attention.

This would happen through the publication of policies and practice which can be read and accessed by interested parties. There will be a duty for the Secretary of State to publish this information on an annual basis.

In Summary

It is obviously vital for people working in educational services to be aware of the legislative framework of their practice. However, since education is an issue for all children and young people it is important for all staff to have some awareness of the legislation and regulations covered in this chapter.

17 THE CHILDREN ACT 1989 AND THE CHILDREN ACT 2004

The Children Act 1989 was the result of a major political climate of child care reform. It replaced most of the child care law which went before it. If you work in child care it is essential that you are very familiar with the Act, and should not rely on this brief guide for your information.

We have referred to parts of the Children Act 1989 in almost every chapter of this book, it is therefore plain to see that this is the major piece of legislation relevant to working with children and young people.

Even though the Act is referred to throughout this book we have chosen to devote a chapter entirely to aspects of the Act.

More recently, the Children Act 2004 is the result of the current political climate in relation to children within society. Again, this Act is referred to in various chapters. However, this chapter will provide an overview of the Act.

Children Act 1989

Layout of the Act

The Children Act 1989 is a major piece of legislation which contains over 100 sections and 15 schedules. It is also supplemented by a range of Guidance notes, regulations etc. The Act is laid out in 12 parts which cover:-

I	Introductory issues
II	Orders with respect to children in family proceedings
III	Local authority support for children and families
IV	Care and supervision
V	The protection of children
VI	Community homes
VII	Voluntary homes and voluntary organisations
VIII	Registered children's homes
IX	Private arrangements for fostering children
XA	Childminding and day care for young children
XI	The Secretary of State's supervisory functions and responsibilities
XII	Miscellaneous and general

Underlying Principles

The Children Act formally introduced several principles which set the tone for work with children and young people. The two most important to consider when assessing the needs of a child are the Paramountcy Principle and Welfare Principle. The Paramountcy Principle set the welfare of the child as being of first importance in an assessment and any subsequent decisions. In too many cases the needs of children had been ignored as workers had seemed to "pander" to the needs of parents. The Welfare Principle is part of the paramountcy principle in that the child's welfare is paramount. Section 1 of the Act contains the Welfare Checklist. This must be referred to when making decisions about a child. It is reproduced below from the original text of the Children Act 1989.

A court shall have regard to:

- (a) the ascertainable wishes and feelings of the child concerned (considered in the light of his age and understanding)
- (b) his physical, emotional and educational needs
- (c) the likely effect on him of any change in his circumstances
- (d) his age, sex, background and any characteristics of his which the court considers relevant
- (e) any harm which he has suffered or is at risk of suffering
- (f) how capable each of his parents, and any other person in relation to whom the court considers the question to be relevant, is of meeting his needs
- (g) the range of powers available to the court under this Act in the proceedings in question

Cultural needs are covered by point (d) as 'background'. Addressing matters of culture and ethnic heritage, disability and social class are not explicit in this checklist but the wording and thoroughness of the checklist is designed to make such matters implicit and a proper assessment made under these headings should cover the issues of a multi-cultural, differently-abled Britain.

Children in Need

The Act makes reference to children in need. The concept of a child in need has three elements. A child may therefore be said to be "in need" where:-

- they are not achieving or maintaining (or being given the
- opportunity to achieve or maintain) reasonable standards of health or development
- there is a significant impairment of health or development
- a child is disabled

The concept of a child in need is intentionally very broad in that, for example, a sibling of a child with a disability can be viewed as a child in need.

If a child is "in need" then the local authority has the power to provide appropriate services.

Local authorities have a duty to identify the extent to which there are children in need within their area, and to publish information for them.

Local authorities also have a duty to open and maintain a register of children with disabilities.

Section 8 Orders

Four orders can be made by the Courts under section 8 of the Act:-

Residence Orders - This is an order which states arrangements for who a child should live with. The person who the child is to live with is not allowed to change the child's name without the consent of everybody who has parental responsibility, nor are they allowed to take the child out of the country for more than a month at a time.

Contact Orders - When a contact order is made the person with whom a child lives must allow the child to have contact with the person named in the order. The Court cannot, however, order the person named to exercise that contact. Contact orders can be made to facilitate and promote contact between a child and any person significant to them. e.g: sibling, grandparent, parent etc. Contact can be direct (e.g.: overnight stays) or indirect (e.g.: telephone conversations, letters etc).

The Court can attach conditions to the contact which could include details about the duration, venue or supervision of contact.

A contact order cannot be made if a child is subject to a care order (see page 138). In this case the local authority has a duty to allow reasonable contact between a child and parent.

Prohibited Steps Orders - A prohibited steps order stops anyone undertaking a particular step with a child without the court's consent e.g: changing a child's school etc.

Specific Issues Orders - This is an order which can be made giving directions to decide a specific question that may arise, or has arisen in terms of any aspect of parental responsibility e.g: What religion should a child be brought up in? What school should a child attend? etc.

Special Guardianship Order

As a result of an amendment introduced by the Adoption and Children Act 2002 new s.14A to s.14G were inserted into the Children Act 1989. These sections relate to the making of a Special Guardianship Order following an application to a court.

The Special Guardian will have parental responsibility in respect of the named child, such that they will not have to consult about decisions relating to the child (unless more than one person is made Special Guardian). [The intention of a Special Guardianship Order is to provide long term stability where adoption is not a suitable alternative].

Family Assistance Orders

Under section 16 of the Act family assistance orders can be made by a court.

Family assistance orders require a probation officer or an officer of the local authority be made available to *advise, assist and befriend* any person named in the order.

The court can specify a period of time up to a maximum of six months. The order cannot be renewed.

These orders were designed to help families where there are disputes over issues such as contact arrangements.

Supervision Orders

People can become confused about supervision orders, since supervision orders can also be made in criminal proceedings under the Crime and Disorder Act 1998.

Under the Children Act 1989 a Supervision Order is an order to enable a local authority to supervise a child. The local authority can require the person responsible for the child to allow access to the child, to notify any change of address etc. In addition conditions can be attached to a supervision order, for example, about where a child should live, be educated etc.

Care Orders

Section 33 of the Act defines the legal effects of a care order. A care order enables the local authority to provide for the child's health and development. It gives the local authority parental responsibility which means that the local authority can make decisions about where the child should live, be educated etc. It also enables the local authority to consent to the child receiving medical/psychiatric assessment and treatment.

Interim Orders

It is very rare that a court is in a position to make either a care order or a supervision order at the first hearing. Section 38 of the Act therefore allows courts to make interim care orders or interim supervision orders, until the court is in a position to make a decision about a full order.

Emergency Protection Orders

Emergency protection orders, as the name suggests, are designed to be used in serious circumstances only. The order is of eight days duration, and in an emergency can be made by a lone magistrate. The order grants the applicant (the local authority) limited parental responsibility and the power to remove or keep safe a child and promote the child's welfare.

To make an emergency protection order the court must be satisfied that the child is at risk of significant harm or is suffering significant harm.

Police Protection

Section 46 of the Act gives the police the power to remove a child or keep a child in a safe place (e.g: hospital) if they have reasonable cause to believe the child is at risk of significant harm.

Education Supervision Orders

These are outlined in section 36 of the Act. An education supervision order relates to children of compulsory school age, placing the child in question under the supervision of a designated local education authority (L.E.A.). The education welfare officer or education social worker allocated to the case then has the duty to *advise, assist and befriend* the child and the parents.

Education supervision orders last initially for one year, but can be extended for up to three years.

Assessment Orders

Section 37 Investigations

Under section 37 of the Act the court has the power to order an investigation of a child's circumstances if it thinks that a care order or supervision order may be appropriate.

Often the local authority is ordered to make the investigation, though a welfare officer could be ordered to do so.

When carrying out the investigation the local authority has to consider whether to apply for a care order or supervision order, whether to provide any services or whether to take any other action.

The local authority has eight weeks to complete a written report for the court.

Child Assessment Orders

A child assessment order can be made under section 43. These are designed to enable an assessment of a child to be made where *significant harm* is suspected, but where the child is not thought to be at *immediate risk*.

The function of this order is to allow an assessment to investigate enough about a child's health and development or the way they are being treated to decide what further action should be taken.

Children Act 2004

The Children Act 2004 provides the legal underpinning for the Every Child Matters: Change for Children Programme.

Layout of the Act

The Act is laid out in 6 parts which cover:

1. Children's Commissioner

2. Children's services in England

    o   General
    o   Local Safeguarding Children Boards
    o   Local authority administration
    o   Inspections of children's services

3   Children's services in Wales

    o   General
    o   Local Safeguarding Children Boards

4   Advisory and support services for family proceedings

5   Miscellaneous

    o   Private fostering
    o   Child-minding and day care
    o   Local authority services
    o   Other provisions

6   General

Underlying Principles

The Act focuses on the outcomes for children outlined in the Every Child Matters Framework. The Act places a duty on services to ensure that every child has the support they need to:

O be healthy

O stay safe

O enjoy and achieve through learning

O make a positive contribution to society

O achieve economic well-being

Nearly twenty years after the 1989 Children Act these underlying principles are as important as the paramountcy principle of that original act. Placing the child at the centre of proceedings is something we take for granted now, but needed to be said in 1989. In the same way, the underlying principles of the Children Act 2004 must be viewed as achievable goals rather than just wispy aspirations. Let us look at some of the 2004 Acts principal measures.

The Children's Commissioner

Essentially the Commissioner's role is in England but also UK wide for non-devolved matters with counterparts in Wales, Scotland and Northern Ireland. The Commissioner's job is to highlight issues that promote the best interests of children and report to Parliament via the Secretary of State.

The Commissioner will not take up individual cases, unless they have wider implications for children nationally or within a specific group. Usually the Commissioner will examine how other bodies, both statutory and private, respond to, and address the needs of children and young people.

Children's Services in England

Section 10 of the Act places a duty on Local Authorities to promote co-operation between agencies to promote children's well-being. This includes the power to combine resources between agencies. This appears to be a refreshing change from rigidly defined budgets and duplication of work by different organisations.

Under section 11, key agencies that work with children and young people have a duty to take account of safeguarding the needs of children and young people when carrying out their functions.

Section 12 allows for secondary legislation to create databases, excluding case details, of children and young people in order to enable agencies to work together and coordinate their efforts. This has resulted in "Contact Point".

Contact Point is a database which holds basic identifying information on every child up to the age of 18. For care leavers or young people with learning disabilities this can be extended to 25 with their consent. Its purpose is to enable the different agencies and professionals working with children to coordinate their efforts and so avoid overlaps or gaps in service provision. This would meet various objectives of the Every Child Matters programme.

Sections 13 to 16 laid out the duties of local authorities to set up Local Safeguarding Children's Boards which followed the abolition of Area Child Protection Committees. The subsequent legislation that regulates these boards are The Local Children Safeguarding Boards Regulations 2006.

Local Authorities, under sections 18 and 19 require local authorities to appoint a Director of Children's Services and Lead Member to take responsibility for Children's Social Services and Education. Local authorities may also add other functions such as Housing or Leisure Services if appropriate.

Bodies with responsibility for inspecting children's services must, under sections 20 to 24, work together within an integrated inspection framework. This should result in regular "Joint Area Reviews" of children's services across local authority areas.

Other Provisions

A strengthened statutory notification scheme for private fostering with the option of further regulation and a registration scheme if these provisions fail. (sections 44-47).

Option to bring in regulations for a minimum fostering allowance. (section49)

Section 50 harmonises inspection of performance, and intervention, between both Education services and Children's Social Services where needed.

Duty on local authorities as Corporate Parents to promote the educational achievement of looked after children. (section 52) Interestingly this is further strengthened in the current Children and Young Person's Bill 2007-2008 which protects and promotes the local placement of looked after children in both residential and educational provision.

In Summary

The Children Act 1989 remains the major statute in terms of working with children and young people. You need to bear in mind that there have been a significant number of amendments to the Act so you need to read the text with the amendments. The fact that the 1989 Act has been amended illustrates how central it still is to children's services. It is therefore vital that you have a detailed understanding of the aspects of the Act that relate to your particular area of practice.

With hindsight, and seen alongside the Children and Young Person's Bill 2007-2008, the 2004 Act is not a fully rounded end-in-itself piece of legislation. It is part of the reforming progression that is the "Every Child Matters" programme. Make no mistake, the 2004 Act makes appropriate and effective changes, but ultimately there is a feeling of waiting for all the pieces of the puzzle to arrive so that we can see the whole picture. Keeping up with changes can, for many practitioners, be discouraging.

18 STANDARDS IN THE CARE OF CHILDREN AND YOUNG PEOPLE

There have been major changes in policy and legislation aimed at safeguarding children and enhancing the quality of services through regulations, national minimum standards, the inspections of services that care for children or provide adoption or fostering services and the creation of organisations or structures that will enhance the quality of services.

This chapter covers:

O Children's Commissioner

O Co-operation between local agencies

O The Regulation and Inspection of Children's Services

O Care Standards Act 2000

O Joint Area Reviews

O General Social Care Council

Towards the end of the chapter, similar issues for readers in Wales are covered.

The Children's Commissioner

The Children Act 2004 establishes the office of Children's Commissioner (s.1). There is a Children's Commissioner for England, a Children's Commissioner for Wales (this office was introduced by the Care Standards Act 2000), a Children's Commissioner for Scotland and a Children's Commissioner for Northern Ireland.

The Children's Commissioner in England has the general task of promoting awareness of the views and interests of children (s.2).

The Children's Commissioner may initiate an inquiry into the case of an individual child if s/he considers that their case raises issues of public policy relevant to other children.

Co-operation Between Local Agencies

Local authorities are given the duty of making arrangements for local co-operation in respect of all services for children. Statutory agencies have a duty to co-operate with the local authority. Integrated commissioning and pooled budgets are made possible (s.10).

The Government wants to see integrated children's services in the form of Children's Trusts. Children's Trusts were originally made possible through the Health Act 1999 (s.31). The Children Act 2004 seeks to accelerate this process.

All statutory agencies must ensure that their services are delivered having regard to the need to safeguard and promote the welfare of children. This duty remains where services are contracted out (s.11).

The local authority has the responsibility to establish a Director of Children's Services and so establish a separate children's department which will integrate education and social services functions for children. A children's department would then co-ordinate local co-operation with other relevant agencies (s.18).

The Secretary of State (Department for Education and Skills) is also given the power to order the appointment of Director of Children's Services which a local authority must comply with (also s.18).

The Regulation and Inspection of Children's Services in England

The Government is actively reforming the organisations that are responsible for inspecting children's services.

There have been many changes in the last 10 years. In 1998 it was recognised in a White Paper (Modernising Social Services, DoH 1998) that the system for inspecting children's services was complicated, different agencies involved and resulted in poor consistency.

Therefore the Government established an organisation called the National Care Standards Commission which was to inspect all children's social care services and adult social care services and some healthcare services. This organisation was established by the Care Standards Act 2000 to start working in April 2002.

The Care Standards Act 2000 also transferred the inspection of child minders and early years nurseries from social services to Her Majesty's Chief Inspector of Schools (which as an organisation is known as Ofsted – Office for Standards in Education).

In mid April 2002 the Government announced it would dissolve the National Care Standards Commission and establish a new inspection agency , the Commission for Social Care Inspection (CSCI). The CSCI has merged with the Social Services Inspectorate (which used to inspect Social Services Departments). All healthcare services were to be inspected by the Healthcare Commission. Hence the CSCI would inspect all social services and social care services (adults and children). As already mentioned, childminding and early years nurseries were inspected by Ofsted.

Every Child Matters called for joint area reviews (inspections) of children's services by some eleven official inspectorates, of which Ofsted and the CSCI were just two. The Government also decided to reduce the number of official inspectorates (partly for cost reasons, partly to reduce overlapping and duplication).

The Government has therefore decided to disband the CSCI. The responsibility for registering, inspecting and reporting on all children's services will rest with Ofsted from April 2007. The legislation to establish this change is in Parliament at the time of writing. This is presently called the Education and Inspections Bill. If the Bill is introduced as the Government wants, then it will result in the establishment of the Office for Standards in Education, Children's Services and Skills.

(The inspection of adult care services will transfer to the Healthcare Commission).

Care Standards Act 2000

Many aspects of the Care Standards Act 2000 are still very relevant even if the registration and inspection agency it introduced was short lived.

The Care Standards Act 2000 introduced the duty on the Secretary of State to generate regulations and National Minimum Standards (NMS) for care services. Each care sector has its own NMS. Hence there are NMS for:

- Children's homes
- Adoption agencies
- Residential family centres
- Fostering services
- Boarding schools
- Residential special schools
- Accommodation of students aged under eighteen by Further Education colleges

Staff in children's services are (and should) be conscious of the importance of the regulations and National Minimum Standards that apply to their service rather than the title of the organisation that an inspector visiting your service belongs to.

Joint Area Reviews in England

The Children Act 2004 establishes the basis for Joint Area Reviews (JAR's) of children's services. JAR's are a broader, strategic assessment of children's services. JAR's are to be conducted jointly between at least two agencies that already inspect services that work with children.

Joint Area Reviews will draw together the results of inspections of individual services as well as reviewing management and organisational aspects of local children's services. A key aspect of JARs is to see how different services are working together.

The lead agency in the review or assessment of children's services is to be the Chief Inspector of Schools.

The organisations that could jointly review children's services include:

O   Chief Inspector of Schools (Ofsted)
O   Commission for Social Care Inspection
O   Chief Inspector of the National Probation Service
O   Chief Inspector of Prisons

The purpose of the review is to evaluate the extent to which the children's services being reviewed improve the wellbeing of children and relevant young people (s.20).

Even when the new enlarged Ofsted starts to inspect all children's services, JARs will continue with the Inspectorates where there still is some overlap (eg. youth offending, police etc).

The General Social Care Council

The Care Standards Act 2000 establishes an agency titled the General Social Care Council. It is the responsibility of this Council to compile registers of social care workers. Due to the high number of workers in this field it will gradually build up its registers. Priorities in its first few years will be:

O   register qualified social workers
O   register staff in children's services
O   register managers of all care homes

To protect the title "social worker" it will become an offence for a person to use this title if they are not registered (s.61).

The General Social Care Council will also have the responsibility of supporting the development and regulation of training for all staff in social care in collaboration with Skills for Care. Additionally the

Council is given the responsibility to issue codes of practice to be followed by all social care workers. This code of practice has been published and is widely available.

The Regulation and Inspection of Children's Services in Wales

The Care Standards Act 2000 gave the Welsh Assembly the responsibility to improve the quality of care services in Wales.

The Welsh Assembly established the Care Standards Inspectorate for Wales (CSIW) [Arolygiaeth Safonau Gofal Cymru (ASGC)] which has the responsibility to register and inspect all provider services (both children and adults) and this includes early years providers (childminders and nurseries).

The Social Services Inspectorate for Wales (SSIW) [Arolygiaeth Gwasanaethau Cymdeithasol Cymru (AGCC)] inspects the social services provided by local authorities and writes reports based on their inspections. The SSIW/AGCC inspections are more of a strategic overview.

Care Standards Act 2000

The Care Standards Act 2000 gave the Welsh Assembly the responsibility to generate regulations and National Minimum Standards for care services. Each care sector has its own National Minimum Standards (NMS). Hence there are NMS for:

- Childrens homes
- Residential family centres
- Residential special schools
- Boarding schools
- Further education colleges that provide accommodation to students under 18
- Fostering agencies
- Child minders
- Crèches
- Daycare

The CSIW/ASGC will actively use the National Minimum Standards when inspecting services for children.

Care Council for Wales/Cyngor Gofal Cymru

This body was established through the Care Standards Act 2000. The Care Council is responsible for:

○ Publishing codes of practice for workers and employers in social care

○ Compiling a register of social care workers

○ Identify the training needs of the social care workforce and promote professional development

○ Regulate social work qualifications, including post qualifying training

The Care Council is seeking to ensure there are high standards of conduct, practice and training for all staff in social care.

 In Summary

Improving the quality of children's services and the outcomes for children in need and looked after children has been an aspiration of the Government for many years. This chapter has outlined the main legislative basis for improving children's services. However, there are other legal obligations that are also relevant – such as supporting care leavers. Additionally, there are many policy initiatives that are important and should be pursued.

19   THE CHILDREN'S PLAN – BUILDING BRIGHER FUTURES, 2007

"We are setting ourselves ambitious new goals for 2020"
Ed Balls, Secretary of State for Children Schools and Families.

It is the Government's intention to "make England the best place in the world to grow up" and the Children's Plan apparently represents a new long term commitment which has its roots and shoots across all areas of Government policy. Six months prior to its release on 11th December 2007 saw the creation of the Department for Schools, Children and Families. Its goal is to have responsibility across Government to ensure that children's issues and the quality of their lives is prioritised.

This chapter covers the essential aspects of the Children's Plan to indicate likely legislative changes in the coming years. All text in quotations is taken from the Children's Plan unless otherwise indicated.

The Children's Plan is the result of a huge consultation program with children, parents, and what the Department terms as "experts". These experts were focused on three areas, 0-7, 8-18 and 14-19 year olds with a central value base that sees children as Young Citizens. From this consultation, the Department formulated six strategic objectives which are:

- Secure the health and wellbeing of children and young people
- Safeguard the young and vulnerable
- Achieve world class standards
- Close the gap in educational achievement for children from disadvantaged backgrounds
- Ensure young people are participating and achieving their potential to 18 and beyond
- Keep children and young people on the path to success

The Children's Plan sets out what the Department is doing to achieve these six objectives.

As well as these six Strategic Objectives, the Children's Plan is underpinned by five value principles and these are:

- Government does not bring up children – parents do – so government needs to do more to back parents and families;
- all children have the potential to succeed and should go as far as their talents can take them;
- children and young people need to enjoy their childhood as well as grow up prepared for adult life;
- services need to be shaped by and be responsive to children, young people and families, not designed around professional boundaries; and
- it is always better to prevent failure than tackle a crisis later.

The Children's Plan stresses the point that the Plan is not an end in itself. It is viewed as the beginning of "a new engagement between Government and Children, Families and Experts."

The Department promises a progress report after one year.

Getting into the Detail

The Plan has seven chapters which follow the six Strategic Objectives. It's not that the maths is off; chapters 3 and 4 split one of the objectives between them. It is worth looking briefly at how the Government hopes to achieve these Strategic Objectives by reviewing those seven chapters.

Chapter 1: Happy and Healthy

Families are seen as "the bedrock of society" so £34 million is to be allocated over the next three years to establish a range of mainstream services to support all parents. These include:

o   Two parenting advisors for every local authority

o   More school based parent support advisors

o   Expand on the current health "Red Book" to provide a personal progress record for children up to primary school age

o   New Parents Panel to advise government policy makers

Families who require "more intensive help" will also receive improved services including outreach from Sure Start centres and a community based key worker scheme. Young carers (children who have to care for parents, siblings or others) are promised extra support. There will also be £60 million allocated over three years to enable children with disabilities to take breaks. The family fund will also be extended to help families of children with disabilities until the child reaches 18.

£225 million will be provided so that Local Authorities can provide safe places for children to play.

A Child Health Strategy will be produced in conjunction with the Department of Health and Child and Adolescent Mental Health Services (CAMHS) will be comprehensively reviewed.

Lastly in this section, there is an ambitious commitment to halve child poverty by 2010 and eradicate it by 2020 in a project with the Department of Work and Pensions. This is to include an action plan in 2008 to reduce overcrowding and a general intention to tackle children's housing needs.

Chapter 2: Safe and Sound

In order to "safeguard the young and vulnerable" the Plan sets out its aims in relation to:

- Risks to children from the Internet and video gaming, concentrating on a review by Dr. Tanya Byron
- The impact of the "commercial world" on children's wellbeing
- Measures to prevent accidents to children in the home.
- Encouragement for local authorities to impose more 20mph zones
- Address bullying by empowering parents of bullied children
- Health and Safety issues for children

Chapter 3: Excellence and Equity

This chapter and one which follows it relate to closing the gap in educational achievement for disadvantaged children.

The proposals are radical and sweeping and are heavily summarised here.

- Greater parental involvement in children's education. A "new relationship" between parents and schools. The Government has pledged to legislate on this "if necessary", so potentially a level of compulsion is implied there
- All children to receive teaching, tailored to their "stage not age", a theme that runs through educational provision in the plan
- £30 million over three years on "Family Learning" to enable parents and carers to "develop skills and learn with their children in schools"
- £100 million over three years to offer free early education and childcare to under 2's in disadvantaged communities

There is also an intention to bolster existing "Every Child" projects – "Every Child a Reader" and "Every Child Counts" (maths) with additional funding:

- £25 million over three years for "Every Child a Writer" to focus on issues of literacy

o   "Age not Stage" tests when the child is ready which would eventually replace Key Stage tests at 11 and 14

o   Measures to address the special needs of "gifted and talented learners"

The Plan also proposes a major review of the Primary curriculum one aspect being the chance for primary children to begin learning one modern foreign language.

Also, £18 million over three years to improve the teaching of children with special educational needs, to be reviewed by Her Majesty's Inspectorate in 2009.

Chapter 4: Leadership and Collaboration

This chapter also aims to bridge the gap in educational achievement for disadvantaged children; this time by reforms within the Education system itself. Again, the proposed reforms and levels of proposed funding seem radical and sweeping. The main intended outcome seems to be the ongoing theme of the personalisation of education and the creation of a "world class" workforce to enable this to happen. £117 million over three years to variously raise the grade of early-care and teaching staff in terms of their respective qualifications. Daycare provision to be graduate managed and teaching qualifications to be raised to a "Master level profession".

The plan proposes to strengthen "Diversity and Collaboration" by requiring every secondary school to have Specialist trust or Academy status and every school to have a "business or university partner" by 2010. A lot of the plan seems very positive but one wonders about the potential for, say; Billaricay-Primary-School-in-association-with-London School of Economics.

This section also reinforces expectations on Local Authorities with regard to failing schools.

Behaviour in the classroom is another big issue that came out of the Government's consultation for the Plan. The use of Behaviour Partnerships is encouraged and it is planned to review their effectiveness while measures for excluded pupils such as "Studio Schools" are proposed.

Buildings, the physical fabric of education provision, are also set for radical review and guidance from Government in terms of their design and carbon footprint. The carbon footprint of schools seem to have nothing to do with standards in education but is perhaps put here to ensure that two important pieces of information about school buildings is in one place. It is presumed that a separate policy document about Schools buildings will appear in due course.

Chapter 5: Staying On

The proposals in this chapter of the Plan intend to ensure that young people are participating and achieving their potential to 18 and beyond.

The main thrust here is to keep young people in education or training for longer, using the following measures:

- Legislation to raise the age of participation in education to 17 in 2013 and 18 from 2015
- 3 New Diplomas in science, humanities and languages
- Create a new independent regulator for qualifications
- Transfer educational funding for 16 to 19 year olds out of the Learning and Skills Council and over to Local Authorities following consultation in 2008
- £31.5 million over three years for disengaged 16 year olds including better tracking and financial incentives

These proposals have triggered much debate and suggestions that a disruptive, disengaged 16 year old who is perhaps bordering on school phobic should be allowed to enter the world of work and helped to do so. It remains to be seen how successful this will be and indeed how it will actually be enacted but the fact that it will be enforced by legislation rather than facilitated by, say, financial incentives does show that the Government is prepared to enact a major cultural change, not just in education but in the daily life of the population.

Chapter 6: On the Right Track

This chapter is subtitled: "Keeping children and young people on the path to success". In effect it is a youth crime policy with a positive spin which is not necessarily a bad thing. It does, however, reflect the general tone of the Plan which assures the reader that things are improving already under this Government and standards are rising. Therefore this chapter reminds the reader that most young people do not offend, which is true of course and counters the often negative image of young people.

The Government seeks to have society focus on the positives, to celebrate the achievements of young people and intends to spend £160 million over two years to improve options for young people in terms of places to go and things to do. Young people should have an "entitlement" to participate in positive activities.

The chapter then turns more to youth offending with the following :

O   £20 million over three years to be spent on Acceptable Behaviour Contracts to compliment Antisocial Behaviour Orders

O   New Drugs Strategy and Youth Alcohol Plan for 2008

O   Review of "Sex and Relationships" education in schools

O   Various other funded measures to tackle youth crime

Chapter 7: Making it Happen: Vision for 21st Century Children's Services

Here, the plan pulls it all together and acknowledges that for its sweeping changes and reforms to occur, change must be "system-wide" and must make sense to those who use its services. Such services must be accessible under one roof in easy to reach places. There must be investment in those who work with children so that society ends up not just with a "safety net for the vulnerable" but a proactive service that is "unlocking the potential in every child".

Building on the ambitions of "Every Child Matters" the Government will expect:

O   Schools to be uncompromising with regard to achievement

O   Children's Trusts to deliver measurable improvements and by 2010 have a system of identification and intervention in place for children "needing additional help". This will be reviewed to see if further legislation is needed to carry it through

O   A Children's Workforce Action Plan to be published in early 2008

Goals for 2020.

In the Plan, the Government has set what it calls "aspirational" goals. There are many and only a small selection are given here.

O   Every child ready for secondary school by age 11
O   Every young person with the skills for adult life by age 19
O   Parents satisfied with the support they receive
O   Employers satisfied with young people's readiness for work
O   Child poverty halved by 2010 and eradicated by 2020

In Summary

If carried out even partially successfully, The Children's Plan would be the biggest single Government engineered package of social reform since the establishment of the National Health Service in 1948. It is very easy to take a cynical view and believe that it will not happen. We cannot tell for sure. However, a more useful area of speculation about this plan is around the specific areas of change that will happen on the way to these proposed goals. Teachers will have to offer still further differentiation (what the Plan calls Personalisation) in the classroom, a skill which many find stressful even now. Showpiece youth facilities will be built and staffed but the Plan has few immediate ideas about how to affect the social shift necessary to get disengaged children and young people to attend them. Schools and individual pupils who looked forward to parting company when the young person reached 16 will soon find they cannot go their separate ways just yet and some commentators are already questioning the wisdom of this.

On the other hand, this is truly an aspirational piece of work and does have many very positive schemes within it, which could make for real, positive change in England today. We must wait and watch.

20 SPECIFIC MISCELLANEOUS LEGISLATION

The preceding chapters of this book have covered pieces of legislation which you need to be aware of both in terms of generic issues and particular areas of work. There are however, some relevant pieces of legislation which have not yet been covered. This chapter will therefore cover a variety of legislation which may be important for your work. The Acts covered are:-

o   Misuse of Drugs Act 1971

o   Mental Health Act 1983

o   Public Interest Disclosure Act 1998

o   Civil Partnership Act 2004

o   Mental Health Act 2007

o   Human Fertilisation and Embryology Bill

Misuse of Drugs Act 1971

This Act is the major piece of legislation in Britain relating to the use/misuse of drugs.

A variety of drugs are listed and categorised into Class A, B or C depending on how harmful the drug is. Any drug which is prepared to be injected is automatically put into Class A. People who possess or supply Class A drugs risk the most severe penalties for drug misuse - ranging from a fine to life imprisonment.

It is important for staff to be aware of this Act because it is an offence under the Act to knowingly tolerate the use of drugs on premises over which you have control. This may therefore be relevant to staff working in any establishment.

Mental Health Act 1983

This is a very wide ranging and complex piece of legislation. We give here only a <u>very</u> brief outline. If you need more information it is important that you refer to the Act as there are a number of complexities within the legislation.

The Act is supplemented by an associated Code of Practice, which is periodically updated.

The definitions of mental disorder which are contained in Section 1 of this Act has been amended by the Mental Health Act 2007 - see later in this chapter.

The Act refers to Approved Social Workers (ASW's) - it states that a local authority must appoint a sufficient number of ASW's and refers to the process of Approving Social Workers under the Act. The ASW role has been reclassified and amended by the Mental Health Act 2007 – see later in this chapter.

The main sections of the Act refer to admissions to hospital. Compulsory admissions can be made to hospital following an application by an Approved Social Worker or the person's *nearest relative*. The nearest relative is not necessarily the person's next of kin and specific details are given in the Act. In practice, the majority of applications are made by ASWs.

In brief a person can be compulsorily admitted to hospital for:-

O   assessment - Section 2 (maximum of 28 days)
O   treatment - Section 3 (maximum six months, renewable for six months and thereafter for one year periods)

The Act also outlines Guardianship orders. These are of six months duration, they can be renewed for six months and thereafter for one year periods. If the application for guardianship is accepted then a named person or a social services department is named as the person's "guardian". The named guardian has the following powers:-

O   to require the person to reside at a specified place
O   to require the person to attend medical treatment occupation, education or training as specified
O   to require access to the person by an ASW, medical practitioner or other specified person

These are the main sections of the Act which make reference to admissions.

However, as stated, there are a number of complex areas covered within the Act. The table below outlines the main sections of the Act, their purpose and duration.

Section Number	Purpose	Duration
2	Admission for assessment	28 days. Not renewable
3	Admission for treatment	6 months. May be renewed for six months, then yearly
4	Admission for assessment in an emergency	72 hours. Not renewable - but can be changed to Section 2.
5 (2)	Doctors holding power	72 hours - Not renewable
5 (4)	Nurses holding power	6 hours. Not renewable but a doctor can change to section 5(2)
7	Reception into guardianship	6 months. May be renewed for 6 months, then yearly
35	Remand to hospital for psychiatric report	28 days, court may renew 28 days at a time up to a maximum of 12 weeks
36	Remand to hospital for psychiatric treatment	As above.
37	Hospital Order (Court)	6 months. May be renewed for 6 months then yearly
135	Warrant to search for and remove a patient	72 hours - not renewable
136	Police power to move a person to a place of safety from a public place	72 hours - not renewable

The Mental Health Act also covers Mental Health Review Tribunals. Each Tribunal consists of legal members, medical members and lay members. Sections 66-78 of the Act refer to tribunals. Basically, however, patients are able to appeal to tribunals at various points during compulsory hospital stays.

The final major area covered by the Act is covered in Section 117. This states that the local health authority and social services have a duty to provide after care services for people for whom the section is relevant. For this reason you may hear people referred to as "Section 117 eligible."

The Mental Health Act is not age specific apart from the provisions in relation to guardianship and supervised discharge. The availability of these two orders is dependent on the patient being 16 or over. Therefore, in theory, at least, children of any age can be detained, assessed and treated under the Mental Health Act. However, there is a historical bias against using the Act in relation to children (Bailey and Harbour 1999).

As can be seen, the Mental Health Act 1983 has been significantly amended by the Mental Health Act 2007 – see later in this chapter.

Public Interest Disclosure Act 1998

This is often referred to as the "whistle-blowers" legislation. It was implemented in July 1999. This Act gives significant statutory protection to employees who disclose malpractice reasonably and responsibly in the public interest and are victimised as a result. If an employee is victimised or dismissed for this disclosure they can make a claim for compensation to an employment tribunal. There is no cap to the amount that can be awarded.

Whilst it is not a statutory requirement there is an expectation that organisations will establish their own whistle blowing policy and guidelines. These guidelines should:

O clearly indicate how staff can raise concerns about malpractice

O make a clear organisational commitment to take concerns seriously and to protect people from victimisation

O designate a senior manager with specific responsibility for addressing concerns in confidence which need to be handled outside the usual management-chain

Staff receive the full protection of the Act if they seek to disclose malpractice responsibly e.g. by following the organisations whistle-blowing policy/guidelines.

If a member of staff goes to the media or police first they only receive the statutory protection if certain conditions are met.

Civil Partnership Act 2004

This Act establishes the right of same sex couples to enter into a civil partnership. This is not a marriage but is a relationship of equivalent seriousness and commitment. The registration of the civil partnership is in a procedure similar to a civil marriage.

Two individuals can enter into a civil partnership if:

- they are of the same sex
- neither is in an existing civil partnership nor presently married
- they are not related to each other in a manner that would bar them from entering into a civil partnership
- they are both 16 or over

Individuals 16 or 17 need their parents permission to enter into a civil partnership. The 2004 Act outlines related responsibilities and rights of a civil partnership eg. occupancy rights etc.

Mental Health Act 2007

This Act received Royal Assent on 19th July 2007. It amends the Mental Health Act 1983 and the Domestic Violence, Crime and Victims Act 2004

This Act amends the legislation governing the compulsory treatment of people with a mental disorder which is laid out in the Mental health Act 1983. The 2007 Act also introduces "deprivation of liberty safeguards" by amending the Mental Capacity Act 2004 in response to the "Bournewood Judgement". It also amends the Domestic Violence Crime and Victims Act 2004 by extending the rights of victims.

The Act covers the covers the territorial areas of the acts it amends – mainly England and Wales, although it also updates legislation for the transfer of patients between all UK areas.

1983 Mental Health Act – Main Changes

O *Definition of Mental Disorder:* applies a new, single definition. The new, simpler definition for the purpose of legislation is "any disorder or disability of the mind". Previous definitions are removed from the 1983 Act. The redundant definitions, now omitted from the 1983 Act are "mental illness, arrested or incomplete development of mind, psychopathic disorder or any other disorder or disability of mind".

O *Young People and Age Appropriate Treatment:* Patients under 18 must be provided with accommodation that is suitable to their age. Duty rests with hospital managers. Also young people aged 16 to 17 who either consent or refuse treatment cannot have their decision overruled by an adult who has parental responsibility for them.

O *Criteria for Detention:* New "Appropriate Medical Treatment" test introduced, meaning that the patient cannot be detained unless appropriate medical treatment is available for them. The old "treatability test" is abolished.

O *Professional Roles:* broadens the range of professionals who can take on the roles previously only carried out by Approved Social Workers (ASW) and the Responsible Medical Officer (RMO). The ASW role is now reclassified as the Approved Mental Health Professional (AMHP) and for this role social workers, nursing staff, occupational therapists or psychologists may be eligible for Approved status. The AMHP assumes the role of initially applying for admission and detention of patients under Part 2 of the 1983 Act. The RMO role is replaced by the Responsible Clinician (RC) also referred to as an "approved clinician" in the 2007 Act. The same group of professionals listed above, in addition to registered medical practitioners, can be approved for this role.

O *Nearest Relative:* new right for patients and county courts to apply to displace the nominated nearest relative. Also, Civil Partners added to the list of relatives.

O *Supervised Community Treatment (SCT):* New for patients following a period of hospital detention. Aimed at tackling the "revolving door" of readmission following treatment failure in the community.

O *Mental Health Review Tribunal:* New power to reduce the time before hospital managers must refer the case to a tribunal. New single tribunal for England.

O *Advocacy:* Independent Mental Health Advocates must be available.

O *Electro Convulsive Therapy:* New patient safeguards are introduced which relate to the patient's ability to consent and to understand the nature and effects of treatment. A patient cannot be given ECT unless they have consented and an approved clinician (or registered medical practitioner if under 18) has certified that they are capable of understanding and giving consent. Where a patient does not have the understanding to give informed consent a registered medical practitioner must certify that the patient is not capable of understanding the nature of the treatment, and that it is appropriate treatment in the circumstances. This must not conflict with any valid "advance decision" (presumably made by the patient in a more lucid moment) or a decision by the Court of Protection.

Mental Health rights is a large area of some people's work and the publishers would advice reviewing the text and guidance of this Act directly if you require further information.

Human Fertilisation and Embryology Bill 2007/2008
UK Wide.
Would Amend Human Fertilisation and Embryology Act 1990

This Bill follows a review of the 1990 Act of the same name.

The 1990 Act regulates the creation, keeping and use of embryos outside the human body. Certain activities are prohibited without a license or prohibited altogether under this Act.

The main purpose of the Bill is to amend the law relating to assisted reproduction treatment and embryo research. It has three parts, covering different areas:

O Part 1: Amendments to the 1990 Act
O Part 2: Makes provision about who is to be treated as the parent of a child who is born as a result of assisted reproduction treatment – meaning the implantation of eggs, sperm or embryos
O Part 3: Miscellaneous and general provisions

Whilst the whole Bill contains interesting legislative changes, those outlined in Part 2 fall best within the scope of this book. They are:

- A woman who has carried a child as a result of the implantation of sperm, eggs or an embryo, and no other woman, shall be treated as the mother of that child. Obviously the transfer of certain rights and responsibilities through adoption still apply

- If a couple, including women in civil partnerships, are participating in treatment together, then the partner of the woman who carries the child is treated in law as the father/other parent of that child. This must, however, be set out in writing with consent given on both sides. This applies even if sperm is donated by a third party

- If the father (within the meaning of this act) dies before the embryo is created, he is still legally the father. This is useful for registering the birth of the child for example. This applies whether or not the man donated sperm

- Sperm donors are not treated in law as fathers of children produced by that process

- As already mentioned, these provisions relate to women in civil partnerships, including situations where the partner parent dies before the birth of the child

- A woman shall not be treated as a parent just because she donated eggs which resulted in the birth of a child

This is a far from simple piece of legislation and a deeper study of the Bill should be made if you are working in this field.

In Summary

Legislation is not written around particular topic areas. Therefore, as we have worked through the knowledge specifications of NVQs and the legislation which we feel you will need to know about there have been some Acts which did not neatly fit into any previous chapter. This chapter has sought to bridge that gap.

CONCLUSION

The legislative basis for children's services has been continually developed and reformed in the last twenty years or so. Legislation and regulations have been used as a tool to improve standards and outcomes for children in Children's services.

It is important that staff have a sense of the legislation that is most relevant to them.

Staff also need to be aware that as well as legislation there are policy initiatives that can be just as important in terms of how staff work on a day to day basis.

It is important to remember that legislation generally relates to minimum standards of practice and good practice is often way ahead of legislation.

REFERENCES

Bailey, S. and Harbour, A. (1999) *Mental Health Act Review: Legislation and the Children Act* (Internet) Department of Health.

Brayne, H. and Carr, H. (2003) *Law for Social Workers* (Oxford) Oxford University Press.

Department of Health (1998) *Modernising Social Services* (London) The Stationary Office

HMSO (2000) *Explanatory Notes to the Care Standards Act 2000* (London) HMSO.

Home Office (1997) *No More Excuses* (London) The Stationery Office.

Home Office (2000) *Domestic Violence: Break the Chain. Multi-Agency Guidance for Addressing Domestic Violence* (Internet) Home Office.

Hughes, H. Parkinson, D. and Vargo, M. (1989) Witnessing Spouse Abuse and Experiencing Physical Abuse: A "Double Whammy"?" *Journal of Family Violence* 4, 197-209.

Thompson, A. (2000) Holy orders *Community Care* 21-27 September.

NVQ UNIT INDEX

NATIONAL OCCUPATIONAL STANDARDS FOR HEALTH AND SOCIAL CARE

Level Three Units (Core and Optional – Children and Young People)

This index details all the NVQ units potentially relevant to work with children and young people. Details are provided on where these units are covered in this book. **NB** Chapters 8 to 20 are relevant to the majority of units, dependent on a candidate's work role and are therefore not particularly referred to in this index.

Unit	Covered in the following chapters of this book	Page Numbers
HSC31	4, 5 and 6	19 to 45
HSC32	4, 5, 6 and 7	19 to 57
HSC33	4, 5 and 6	19 to 45
HSC34	4, 5, 6, 7, 8 and 9	19 to 73
HSC36	4, 5, 6 and 7	19 to 57
HSC37	4, 5, 6 and 7	19 to 57
HSC38	4, 5, 6 and 7	19 to 57
HSC39	4, 5, 6, 7 and 16	19 to 57 and 119 to 132
HSC310	4, 5, 6, 7 and 14	19 to 57 and 107 to 110
HSC311	4, 5, 6, 7 and 14	19 to 57 and 107 to 110
HSC312	4, 5, 6, 7 and 14	19 to 57 and 107 to 110
HSC313	4, 5, 6 and 7	19 to 57
HSC314	4, 5, 6 and 7	19 to 57
HSC315	4, 5, 6 and 7	19 to 57
HSC316	4, 5, 6 and 7	19 to 57
HSC317	4, 5, 6 and 9	19 to 45 and 65 to 73
HSC318	4, 5, 6 and 9	19 to 45 and 65 to 73
HSC319	4, 5, 6 and 7	19 to 57
HSC320	4, 5, 6 and 7	19 to 57
HSC321	4, 5, 6 and 7	19 to 57
HSC322	4, 5, 6, 7 and 13	19 to 57 and 97 to 105
HSC323	4, 5, 6, 7 and 11	19 to 57 and 81 to 88
HSC324	4, 5, 6, 7 and 13	19 to 57 and 97 to 105
HSC325	4, 5, 6, 7, 9 and 11	19 to 57, 65 to 73 and 81 to 88
HSC326	4, 5, 6, 7 and 9	19 to 57 and 65 to 73
HSC327	4, 5 and 6	19 to 45

Level Three Units (Generic Optional Units)

Unit	Covered in the following chapters of this book	Page Numbers
HSC343	4, 5, 6 and 7	19 to 57
HSC344	4, 5, 6 and 7	19 to 57
HSC345	4, 5, 6 and 7	19 to 57
HSC346	4, 5, 6 and 7	19 to 57
HSC347	4, 5, 6 and 7	19 to 57
HSC348	4, 5, 6 and 7	19 to 57
HSC349	4, 5, 6 and 7	19 to 57
HSC350	4, 5, 6 and 7	19 to 57
HSC351	4, 5, 6 and 7	19 to 57
HSC352	4, 5, 6 and 7	19 to 57
HSC356	4, 5, 6, 7, 9 and 14	19 to 57, 65 to 73 and 107 to 110
HSC360	7	47 to 57
HSC361	7	47 to 57
HSC364	4, 5 and 6	19 to 45
HSC366	4, 5, 6 and 7	19 to 57
HSC367	4, 5 and 6	19 to 45
HSC368	4, 5 and 6	19 to 45
HSC369	4, 5, 6 and 7	19 to 57
HSC370	4, 5, 6 and 7	19 to 57
HSC371	4, 5, 6 and 7	19 to 57
HSC372	4, 5, 6 and 7	19 to 57
HSC373	4, 5, 6 and 7	19 to 57
HSC375	7	47 to 57
HSC379	7	47 to 57
HSC382	4, 5, 6 and 7	19 to 57
HSC383	4, 5, 6 and 7	19 to 57
HSC384	4, 5 and 6	19 to 45
HSC385	4, 5, 6 and 7	19 to 57
HSC387	4, 5, 6 and 7	19 to 57
HSC388	4, 5, 6 and 7	19 to 57
HSC389	4, 5, 6, 7 and 9	19 to 57 and 65 to 73
HSC393	4, 5, 6 and 7	19 to 57
HSC394	4, 5, 6, 7 and 9	19 to 57 and 65 to 73
HSC395	4, 5, 6, 7 and 9	19 to 57 and 65 to 73
HSC398	4, 5, 6, 7 and 9	19 to 57 and 65 to 73
HSC3100	4, 5, 6 and 7	19 to 57
HSC3101	4, 5, 6 and 7	19 to 57
HSC3102	4, 5, 6 and 7	19 to 57
HSC3103	4, 5, 6 and 7	19 to 57
HSC3110	4, 5, 6 and 7	19 to 57

Level Three Units (Additional)

Unit	Covered in the following chapters of this book	Page Numbers
HSC3111	4, 5, 6 and 7	19 to 57
HSC3112	4, 5, 6 and 7	19 to 57
HSC3114	4, 5, 6, 7, 10 and 14	19 to 57, 75 to 79 and 107 to110
HSC3115	4, 5, 6, 7 and 9	19 to 57 and 65 to 73
HSC3116	4, 5, and 6	19 to 45
HSC3117	7	47 to 57
HSC3118	7	47 to 57
HSC3119	4 and 5	19 to 40
HSC3121	4, 5, 6 and 7	19 to 57

Level Four Units (Core and Optional – Children and Young People)

Unit	Covered in the following chapters of this book	Page Numbers
HSC41	4, 5, 6 and 9	19 to 45 and 65 to 73
HSC42	4, 5, 6, 7 and 9	19 to 57 and 65 to 73
HSC43	4, 5, 6 and 18	19 to 45 and 145 to 151
HSC44	4, 5, 6, 8, 16, 18 and 19	19 to 45, 59 to 63, 119 to 132 and 145 to 160
HSC46	4, 5, 6, 8 and 18	19 to 45, 59 to 63 and 145 to 151
HSC47	4, 5, 6, 8 and 18	19 to 45, 59 to 63 and 145 to 151
HSC48	4, 5, 6, 7, 10, 11 and 18	19 to 57, 75 to 88 and 145 to 151
HSC49	4, 5, 6, 7, 9 and 18	19 to 57, 65 to 73 and 145 to 151

Level Four Units (Generic Optional Units)

Unit	Covered in the following chapters of this book	Page Numbers
HSC413	4, 5, 6, 7, 9 and 18	19 to 57, 65 to 73 and 145 to 151
HSC414	4, 5, 6 and 7	19 to 57
HSC415	4, 5, 6, 7, 9 and 18	19 to 57, 65 to 73 and 145 to 151
HSC416	4, 5, 6, 7, 9 and 18	19 to 57, 65 to 73 and 145 to 151
HSC417	18 and 19	145 to 160
HSC418	6 and 18	41 to 45 and 145 to 151
HSC419	6 (and others dependent on role)	41 to 45
HSC420	7 and 18	47 to 57 and 145 to 151
HSC423	6, 7 and 9	41 to 57 and 65 to 73
HSC425	4, 5, 6, 7 and 9	19 to 57 and 65 to 73
HSC429	4, 5 and 6	19 to 45
HSC430	4, 5, 6, 7 and 9	19 to 57 and 65 to 73
HSC431	4, 5, 6, 7 and 9	19 to 57 and 65 to 73
HSC433	4, 5, 6, 7, 9 and 18	19 to 57, 65 to 73 and 145 to 151
HSC435	4, 5, 6, 10, 11 and 18	19 to 45, 75 to 80 and 145 to 151
HSC436	18	145 to 151
HSC446	6 and 18	41 to 45 and 145 to 151
HSC449	18	145 to 151
HSC450	4, 5, 6, 7 and 9	19 to 57 and 65 to 73
HSC451	4, 5, 6, 7 and 9	19 to 57 and 65 to 73

Level Four Generic Additional Unit

Unit	Covered in the following chapters of this book	Page Numbers
HSC452	4, 5, 6, 7 and 9	19 to 57 and 65 to 74

INDEX TO LEGISLATION